A Slave Insurrection

By Bertrand Brown

ISBN-13: 978-1511533249
ISBN-10: 1511533242

Part One

Ever since I can remember I been a slave. I ain't liked it but that's the lot I bore in life. Still, it don't mean that I gotta like it. I was fortunate though that is if you can believe there can be any good fortune in servitude. I was born of two very proud Africans who refused to believe they were any less than their white captors and slave holders. Being that they were both very religious they believed that this was there penance, their cross to bear. They were no dummies though. They realized that any kind of ruckus and we'd be split up as a family and so they went about their work quietly and efficiently never making any waves.

My mama and pappy were the only married couple that had been a married couple and made the journey and still somehow remained together but somehow they did and I think this gave them an advantage over most. They had the old traditions and ways, the old time religion, the language but most of all they had each other. So, no matter what the master threw their way it didn't faze them as long as they knew they could rely on each other. And in their union there was strength. My pappy was the blacksmith for the Three Winds Plantation and soon was the blacksmith for all Jackson County. I was what he called his apprentice and soon was as good if not better than he was.

My pappy used to always say that the more you knew the more value you would be to the massa and since that's all white folks valued was money then the less likely he would be to strike you or do other vile things to you and those belonging to you. He said that's why massa ain't never struck him or his children. As long as he was blacksmithing and putting a hefty sum in massa's pocketbook massa didn't mess with him. Still, and all this wasn't enough for my pappy and over the years he formed a secret council of some of the more respected and loyal slaves not only on Three Winds Plantation but in all of Jackson County.

In all, there were close to three hundred slaves in the council. Pappy used to say that for now it was all about our survival but in time the council would have another purpose and they were simply biding their time.

In the meantime we should accrue all the knowledge of our captors and the way they went about things that we could. And this knowledge would one day lead to our eventual freedom and self-sufficiency.

I can remember being a very small lad playing in the front yard in front of the big house with massa's son John when John's mama Missy Mary Anne called him in. He left crying and in a few minutes she was back summoning me. I went and soon found myself in the library seated next to John. Now Miss Mary Anne was a northerner who massa had met a few years prior on a business trip. The two had fallen head over heels in love and soon married despite Miss Mary Anne being a fervent abolitionist. And though they had frequent arguments over slavery she loved him enough to overlook the fact that he was one of the biggest slavers in Jackson County.

Despite her attempts to overlook his transgressions pappy said things would have been a hell of a lot worse had missy never appeared on the scene. I couldn't see how. Niggras was being whipped every day for something or another. In any case she had a hard time getting John to do

2

anything if I wasn't in his company so she had me sit there as she taught him to read and write and taught me too. Truth be told, I had a much easier

time of it than John did and would more often than not turn to him when his mother could not get through to him. In any case, when mama who worked in the big house as cook and maid told my pappy this he couldn't stop grinning and before you knew it I was not only teaching mama and daddy to read and write but the most trusted members of the council as well. Pappy saw this as an invaluable tool and I soon came to realize why it was that niggras had been forbidden to read or write but thanks to Missy Mary Anne who fed me every book I took an interest in I became a voracious reader reading everything from Alexander the Great to Machiavelli. It taught me a lot about how the white man thought and what he thought of me.

When I was about thirteen I'd read much of massa' library without his ever knowing and mama would sneak books out every evening in addition to what Missy Mary Anne would feed me. And I hardly talked anymore for fear that some of what I had learned would come out but every week when the Eastern Clarion newspaper would come out I'd make John read it to me before we'd do anything else and then would repeat all the news out of Jackson to my pappy that evening. If there was any news that he felt would affect us niggras he would summon the council and have them act on it after dark.

When I was thirteen my pappy told me he wanted to have a long talk with me. I couldn't imagine why since I'd already made my way around the quarters once or twice with most of the gals my age or a little older.

Later that night I was surprised that he called me after dinner. This was my time for reading and he usually insisted that I spend my time in this manner. The quarters were quiet for the most part and everyone had pretty much settled in for the night. Massa Nicholson, the ovaseer had made his rounds when pappy called for me to go with him.

We walked for close to an hour through the woods until we reached a small clearing where ten or eleven men my father's age had gathered. They greeted him warmly in a tongue I had only heard when my folks

3

were saying something they didn't want me to hear. But here in this clearing of poplars they all seemed familiar with it.

Most of the men I knew or at least seen from time-to-time in the shadows of the night. To those I didn't know he introduced me before sitting. Two men with old rusty shotguns stood watch. My father sat and the men talked and laughed for a while passing a jug of homemade hooch. Of this I was offered none and then they smoked as if they were once again enjoying the sunny beaches of the Gold Coast I'd heard so much about until my father called them to attention. The mood suddenly changed and all was serious.

From what I gathered from the ensuing conversation two slaves, a father and son had been hunting over on the O'Reilly Place. Slavers by the name of Heathcliff and Clinton had come across the two men. The father commenced to tell the slavers that it had been a lean winter and he was simply trying to find some game to feed his wife and four children. Heathcliff not believing the slave's story decided a whipping was in order

for this lying niggra and when the slave resisted by struggling and pleading Heathcliff became so enraged that he shot the man and then hung him. When the slave's son pleaded with the slaver to spare his father's life he too was shot and hung.

This was not been the first incident of these two slavers hanging slaves who hadn't been runaways and it was quickly decided by the council that something had to be done.

The men surrounding my father at the council showed no fear or hesitation in coming to a plan of action and only looked to my father as the head of the council to give the final word which he did with a simple nod of his head and the plans were soon drawn up as to who would carry out the actual act. Being that it had taken place over by the O'Reilly Plantation two of O'Reilly's slaves would handle the fate of the two slavers and Ol' Ben who chaired that particular branch of the council was to make sure it was carried out and inform the council when they convened the following week.

I was amazed. I had never seen niggras, slaves, men like me, (although I was not quite a man yet), act with such daring, with such cunning, strength and decisiveness. And in my eyes my pappy was the chief, the general and I gained a new found respect. I likened my pappy to Alexander the Great, and Hannibal.

Yes my father, my very own father was a general, a leader of men commanding respect and working under the guise of a lowly slave, a niggra shuffling at massa's every command. Who knew?

I was in the midst of an epiphany. When the council meeting was over and it was decided that the judge who condoned the murders and was and had been on the side of these slavers more than once had to go too I was fit to be tied. My father who could see my unbridled adoration spoke to me in the calm nurturing tone he always had. Slowly and calmly as if he was helping me to walk for the first time he explained to me the task at hand and said it was not easy or simple to act as judge and jury and deliberate over a man's life but in order to avoid us all being killed we could not stand idly by. And he and only he would have to stand up to God's wrath in the end but he would do that if it meant him having to save many an innocent life now. And as young as I was I understood. I also understood that he was grooming me to be a leader in much the same way he was.

From that day on, I was not a young lad anymore. My whole disposition changed. I was serious about everything now, about all of my undertakings. I read and worked as if my very life depended on it. I wanted to be able to make my father proud in succeeding him and many a night when the quarters were sleep and only the lonesome owl could be heard in the distance he and I talked and strategized about how to best serve and save our people from a system that was doomed to kill us all.

In the end we came to the mutual agreement and understanding that we would never be able to confront our adversary head on. Though we far outnumbered them we were far to the disadvantage in every other aspect.

No, it would take brains and sly cunning if were to make it a battle and even then it could not be a widespread offensive. No, our goal was to take plantation by plantation. And that's what we set out to do.

Little did I know that the battle had long ago been waged and that I was just the latest recruit. How a slave could not or would not join the ranks of this most holy order I could not fathom but my father assured that the council and its teachings had to remain a secret as many a slave in their ignorance held an allegiance to their owners. It all seemed ludicrous but I'd already witnessed more times than I'd like to remember slaves telling on each other hoping to gain the favor of massa. So, I had no problem keeping the whole affair secret. More importantly it gave me a sense of belonging to an elite group and I liked that.

In the weeks that followed I could see no difference. Massa relied heavily on my pappy and my pappy continued to work just as hard and diligently and even harder at night with the council. He and mama had become pretty proficient readers by this time and had taught many members of the council to read and write which allowed them to write out passes enabling them to flee North to freedom or carry out the business of the council right there in Jackson.

Times were tough for us slaves right through there. With Nat Turner's slave insurrection white folks was on high alert but a niggra with a pass thought to be carrying out his massa's work was pretty much at liberty to go as he pleased. This was a great help to the council and enabled them to carry out most of their work without the constant fear of being apprehended. When the two slavers were found hanging in plain view near the O'Reilly Plantation. Ol' Ben and Zeus were both questioned. Ben pulled out their traveler's passes and the two slaves were immediately allowed to pass and nothing else was ever thought of it since everyone knew that niggras couldn't read let alone write.

Little did the authorities know that it was Ol' Ben who had actually arranged the execution of the two slavers Heathcliff and Clinton. You see it was well-known that the two slavers had a penchant for niggra wenches and Ol' Ben who had as much clout and authority on the O'Reilly Plantation as my daddy did at Three Winds got one of his most trusted niggra gals by the name of Ofay and spelled out the plan to her.

Now Ofay had been previously accosted and raped by the two slavers so she wasn't averse to seeing them pay for their transgression. So when Ol 'Ben had worked out all the details he had the comely, young woman

6

stand by the road at exactly ten o'clock which by Zeus' calculation was the time the two would leave Ms. Flaherty's Pub.

On this particular night Ofay walked the dusty, dirt road on her way back to the O'Reilly Plantation carrying a bushel basket of clean clothes. Two horsemen approached. The one on the gray and white dun was immediately recognizable. And it

didn't take the young woman to see that it was none other than Heathcliff the slaver. Alongside of him on the old brown mare rode Heathcliff's sidekick Clinton. It was easy to see that both men were drunk and ready for mischief.

"Whatcha got dere nigga?"

"Nothin' but m'massa's clean laundry," Ofay stuttered.

"You got a pass nigga?" Heathcliff said approaching slowly.

"No, suh. I neva has a pass when I go to do massa's laundry ova ta da creek. Massa neva see fit ta give me one suh. I's jes goin' ta da creek."

"Well, we'll jes see about that you black wench," Heathcliff said stepping down from his horse.

Ofay dropped the basket and took flight into the woods. It was dark but she'd been through the woods more times than she could remember. Hot on her heels were the two slavers and when she fell in the clearing they were on her immediately.

"Wouldn't do that if I was you boy," Ol' Ben said stepping from the trees. Slaves from all directions formed a circle around the slavers and the now smiling young woman.

"This whatch'all get," Ofay shouted at the drunken white men. "You can't just go around shootin' and rapin' innocent gals and think you gonna go unpunished. This ain't

7

nothin' but the wrath of God layin' his hands on you suh. This here is judgment day for you crackers."

Heathcliff ignored her.

"I don't know what you niggas is thinkin' but y'all better get the hell outta here and back where you belong before me and Mr. Clinton get ta havin' a lil necktie party of our own," Heathcliff said still staring at the girl and smiling.

Ol' Ben moved closer to the slaver his face stern. There was no play in it. The next words that came from his mouth were chilling and both slavers now turned their eyes from the girl and focused on the tall, tawny, niggra that stood before them.

"The only hangin' party that's gonna take place tonight is yours suh."

"Why nigga…"

"Muzzle this fool," Ben said to no one in particular. Four men emerged from the shadows and took hold of the two slavers. Heathcliff tried to struggle, cursing mightily at the two men now wrestling with him when Zeus appeared leading their horses into the clearing. Handing the horses to the girl he approached the struggling slaver hit him once ending the struggle and silencing the man.

"Ofay?"

The young woman stepped up and eased each man's trousers to the ground. Once she had them off she tied their legs together at the ankles. Already bound to the same willow tree there wasn't much either could do than to await their fate.

Zeus then led each man's horse before them and slowly and meticulously took out his bowie knife and slashed their throats. The tears rolled down both men's eyes. This had become a customary practice prior to any execution by the council because it was understood that in the white man's eyes even before his wife and children he valued his horse.

8

Ofay sat a few feet away sharpening her razor and humming the old gospel hymn, Closer My God to Thee. When both horses lay dead at their owner's feet only then did Ofay approach the men. She too went about the task at hand slowly and methodically.

"You will never rape another niggra," she commented aloud as she sliced slivers of meat from their genitals. Their screams muffled by the cloth muzzling them they writhed and twisted in pain. Ofay continued not affected in the least by the torture of these men.

She like most slaves had long ago grown immune to the sight of blood or emotional pain. When they could take no more and were seemingly on the verge of losing consciousness she came down in one sweeping motion cutting off each man's penis and awakening them to a new pain. Their eyes all but bulged out of the sockets as

they now writhed and squirmed in excruciating pain. In this condition they were allowed to suffer in pain for a good half an hour when Ol' Ben walked up and shot each man point blank before hanging them.

That was a slave's justice and though I understood the necessity for it I never took any pleasure in administering such a cold, calloused thing as taking another man's life whether he be niggra or white. But carry out the council's work I did and I take no pride in telling you that I was proficient in my duties when it came to killing and quickly rose through the ranks leaving little question as to who would be my father's rightful successor.

My first duty as a member of the council was to teach my people to read and once the lights went out I'd meet with my fellow slaves every night in someone's cabin where I'd be met by four or five other slaves with a hankering to learn to read. Reading was against the law for niggras at the time and could easily get you twenty or more lashes but with Miss Mary Anne being so strong an abolitionist I do believe that if I'd been caught she would have foregone the punishment but we was still careful in our undertaking. And the idea of a slave running and telling was pretty much a foregone conclusion. Most of the slaves respected and feared my father. They didn't know about the council but they knew he had some power amongst the slaves and those that fell out of favor either wound up dead or disappearing so we didn't have to fear that. They also know that he was massa's favorite so to tell on him or anyone associated with him could only bring the

wrath upon you.

Me, I enjoyed teaching my brethren but I enjoyed the fringe benefits even more. Most of my students during this time were women who were so grateful that I was teaching them to read and write that they insisted on paying me with what little they had.

On most nights I would go home with tins of biscuits, pies and crumpets. Many of the women who were unable to pay in this manner or had little time to bake while caring for their younguns simply gave of me themselves which at fifteen or sixteen years of age I deemed more than ample payment.

All was going well when massa decided that pappy was doing so well at blacksmithing that he would open up a blacksmith and tannery in Jackson which was some ten miles away. And just like that massa took m'pappy who had been so instrumental in me growing into a man away and making me the lone blacksmith for Three Winds.

Ten miles wasn't very far away but for a boy that adored his father and clung on to his every word this was tantamount to murder and once again things grew clearer to me. It didn't matter that my father had a family or a son that adored him. All that was clear to massa was that he had a source of income and he would place m'pappy where it would best serve him to make more money for he and his family to enjoy as if he didn't have enough money as it was.

My poor mother who slaved in the big house was heartbroken. She had never been apart from her husband and now this. My pappy being the man that he was assured us that he would be home on the weekends and although we heard him we knew that he wasn't the one calling the shots. And just as I expected pappy's profiency in his trade was his and our undoing. Business was better than could be expected and he worked long hours and the better part of the weekend trying to keep up with the now expanding trade.

For a while I stood in for my father at council meetings but when it became apparent that his duties would not allow him to continue I was elected the new council head. And because of the profound affect slavery had on me and my father's forced exile I vowed to take the council in a new and harsher direction. My mother could see the difference in me and spoke to my father about me on the rare occasions she now saw him. I was eighteen or nineteen by this time and filled with a vindictive rage. My father knowing me as he did understood my anger. There wasn't a slave out there that didn't understand my anger and outrage that lived under this maniacal system of slave and master.

At nineteen I was so full of hatred and pessimism that I sometimes woke up in a cold sweat as I fought to control my anger. I began to recruit members to the council that thought and felt as I did and it was only my father's words and calming presence that tempered my anger so I could continue on somewhat of an even keel. I grew ever more morose and the older members seeing my overwhelming penchant and zest for blood as

potential for suicide began to withdraw electing to step down from the council and turn it over to the younger members who now made up the majority. We were bloodthirsty and in whites that travelled the roads alone at night were prone to be robbed and lynched and fed to the alligators in the nearby swamps.

One evening not long after I met with my father. It was I not my mother who massa chose to meet with my father on a somewhat regular basis but it was not out of compassion for a family now broken and split. It was only because the work had become almost overwhelming for my pappy who had aged somewhat dramatically after being taken from his wife of forty years. When the work was finished my father took me aside.

11

"Son, the idea of war is imminent. Any day now Lincoln will declare war on the South. There is talk and every day I see men preparing for the inevitable. The South cannot win. They neither have the manpower nor the industry to hold off the North. It will be a sad day for the white man but it is a day that was destined to come. There will be much sorrow and much bloodshed. And there is no good that can come of it aside from our freedom and so I say let there be war. But the backlash for slaves will be horrendous to say the least. Angry southerners will blame us for the turmoil and the countless deaths. But as in slavery we must look past his transgressions and continue to work to build ourselves into a nation of thinkers and doers. We must do as we have always done. We must make progress in spite of. And when it all becomes a bit too much and we are threatened with lethargy on our part and overwhelming brutality on his

then and only then should we use the council to act as an intermediary and level the playing field. Then and only then will we still be held with honor and respect in our fellow man's eye and in God's. Indiscriminate violence in the name of retribution for ungodly acts of violence committed against us make us his ally in violence and sin. That is not why we were founded. And although we grow incensed by his actions we do want not to emulate him. We are a distinct people of color of another culture that does not condone violence. We, in fact abhor it but we will and can resort to it when it comes to protecting our families and our way of life.

But let me not digress my son. You are a good man and a better son. Do not let your anger make you bitter and change your heart. You are angry for what massa has done to your family. You want to seek retribution but you have let the devil control your spirit. You, my son have stopped thinking. You have stopped using the gifts that he has given you to traverse this thing called slavery. You have lost your perspective and without those you cannot win your war with your captors. He may not have superior might to beat the North but he has the might to beat a lowly group of slaves. You cannot fight with emotion clouding your vision. You must use your superior intellect, your cunning and your wisdom. Don't speak. Listen and find the chinks in their armor. Then exploit his weaknesses and in time you will hold the keys to the kingdom. Just be patient and bide your time. Do you understand me son?"

I nodded. To his credit my father, a lowly slave was every bit as wise as Socrates and Plato and I implored any man including Lincoln to challenge his wisdom.

"Today is the day you change your tactics from solely retribution and reprisal against the continuing ills of the slave society to a doctrine for the upliftment for a people about to be caste out with nothing once the war is over. Prepare for life less the shackle that bind and give them purpose. Give them land and make them self-sufficient and ease the transition from slave to freedmen. I want you to concentrate the majority of the council's efforts on moving us forward as a people."

I worked alongside of my father that day for the last time as he handed over the mantle and the keys to the kingdom. I left him late that evening. He gave me his customary hug but I noticed something different in his demeanor. His shoulders drooped and he looked sad and worn. This man who stood like the mountains in my eyes no longer stood tall and proud like the African kings he told me stories of when I was just a youngster. No. Something was amiss and though I couldn't exactly pinpoint what it was it bothered me so that I went to my mother's cabin and shared the change in my father.

Early the next morning I was awakened by a lone rider. From the unevenness of the gallop I quickly recognized Massa Nicholson's horse.

"Massa wants you to head to Jackson. Seems yo' pappy kicked off during the night. He's gonna need you to man the blacksmith shop from here on out. Tell yo' mammy she can take the buckboard and one of the field hands into Jackson and pick up his body if she's a mind too or I can send word to the city to pick up the body. Tell her to

let me know either way. I'll be down in the lower forty," he said turning and galloping off.

13

I could feel the blood dripping from the palms of my hands as I clenched so tightly that my nails dug into my flesh. How could anyone be so cold and unfeeling?

It had been a long time since I'd let my emotions get the best of me but they did that morning as mama and I leaned and cried on each other's shoulders for the entire ten mile ride into Jackson. Alas slavery had killed my pappy as well. And now I understood why he'd asked me not to seek retribution going forward. If it had not been for his wishes last night I could have started with that bastard who had just informed me of my father's passing. The thought still ran through my mind but he too would serve his purpose and his day too would come.

My father and I had spoken of the ovaseer on occasion and it was my father's wisdom that had calmed my overzealous nature and tempered my anger when Massa Nicholson had whipped Petunia on massa's orders for slackin' in the field. I'd spent the previous night with Petunia and knew the reason why my pretty little honeydew wasn't up to par. I told my pappy and he smiled.

"And you're angry with massa for whipping yo' gal when you know that whatever you do the night befo' ain't got nothing do with massa's expectations for her today. Gal had a job to do and didn't meet the expectations and that's Massa Nicholson's fault? He gotta job to do just like you and me. Don't shoot the messenger for your indiscretions. If anybody shoulda been whipped it shoulda been you for settin' that po' gal up. As far as ovaseers go Massa Nicholson is betta than most on account he po' lazy, white trash and ain't gonna do no mo' than he has to. He ain't whippin' no niggras unless massa tell 'em to. His laziness is our blessin'," pappy said with a smile.

With no more than a word I could have had Massa Nicholson dragged off into the nearby swamps and had him strung up and castrated but I had to refrain from letting my emotions getting the best of me. I had to bide my time and carry out my father's wishes.

With cunning and strategy I had to formulate a plan for my folks in lieu of their impending freedom. In my head and in my heart I knew that no war and no legislation was gonna affect the southern attitude. If anything they

14

would dig in and fight harder after Lincoln decreed us free. We had to have a plan. We had to be ready.

The talk of war looming just over the horizon was no longer just conversation and in the coming weeks I watched Jackson mobilize. Our worked continued but the emphasis was no longer on us but on the impending war. We were not asked—for obvious reasons—to be a part of the war effort for fear that we would sabotage any Confederate efforts and most of the white men that were of any account were forced to join the war effort. Our impending freedom lay in the balance and I heard my pappy's words resounding like the Liberty Bell on Independence Day.

It was kind of ironic to me though that the South who understandably did not trust the niggra to be a part of the impending war effort in any shape or form would leave his

family to the mercy of us slaves who he had beaten and whipped and emasculated for more than a century. I, however, did not question their logic and tearfully waved goodbye as my friend and loving massa, Massa John was commissioned a colonel and went off to fight to keep me enslaved.

Missy Mary Anne, Massa John's new wife had come to love me and entrust in me the same way her husband had and in seeing her new husband go off to war she buried her tear-stained face in my shoulder and told me that I would have to now be responsible for carrying the majority of the weight of running Three Winds in her husband's absence. I didn't know what would be any different. The blacksmithing in Jackson had long ago come to a close and I'd been back at Three Winds looking after mama and many of the single women and fatherless children as well as the place for a couple of years now along with my role as blacksmith and chief of the council. So, this was nothing new but without the colonel around I had more of a free reign as to what took place amongst us colored folks and took a more hands on approach with the field hands in an attempt to make their work easier and the crop yield more productive and in acquiring these skills now the transition later to cultivating their own lands would be that much easier.

You see I had a plan and while Massa Nicholson was down in the lower forty sitting under the shade of the old willow doing his best to keep cool while the slaves toiled in the hot July sun I puttered back and forth from barn and the blacksmith shop keeping an ear out for anything concerning the war. Missy Mary Anne who was totally dejected by this time had lost all faith in everything and was content to let me and her

ovaseer run the place and he being a lazy, shiftless bastard was content to simply laze around and save his energy for the evenings when he would come down to the quarters and choose a wench and take 'em back to the barn where he would have his way with them.

I, on the other hand had conceived a plan that I considered fool proof with just a little luck.

By this time, I had read a good of the medical journals and following my father's passing I had spoken to mama and rehearsed her on her grief and her unwillingness to live. And this she presented to Miss Mary Anne in the weeks following my father's death. I have to admit mama's act was spectacular to say the least. Of course the woman was in the throes of a grief like I have never witnessed and would never like to witness again. Morose and lethargic, Missy Anne questioned me about mama.

"Andrew. Do you have a minute? I'd like to speak to you concerning your mama," she said as she sat on the veranda overlooking the back yard sipping her customary Mint Julep.

"Yes, mam," I responded in the traditional slave manner I'd been taught staring at the ground in front of me.

"Your mother doesn't seem to be the same ol' Lizzy Mae. She's despondent. She just sits staring for long periods of time. She doesn't respond when I call her? She's

well—just not the same ol' jovial Lizzy Mae that I'm used to. Is there something wrong that I don't know about?"

It was times like these that I wanted to ask God why he put this curse upon us. Could she possibly be so calloused and unfeeling? Was she simply devoid of all thought? But I knew somewhere down deep that this thing called servitude was simply our cross to bear and that as sure as there was a God that ruled the heavens and the earth that he would free us from this bondage.

Miss Mary Anne stared at me waiting for a response.

"Ma'am I'm not sure if you're aware of it or not but my pappy, her husband of thirty-five years passed away not more than three weeks ago. She's grievin' and hasn't been the same since. She sits and just mutters to herself now. Always talkin' about ending it all now. She doesn't cook or wash or anything anymore and if I don't take her to relieve herself she will sit right there and go on herself. She's really in a bad way. Nowadays when I have to work late into the evening Aunt Mamie comes to take care of her. I been meaning to speak to you about it."

"Oh my goodness! You don't say. I never realized that you people grieved like that. I thought it was just white people that had those feelings. I am so sorry to hear that. Well, Andrew what do you suggest I do? I mean I can't just have her sitting around like a retard. Her whole demeanor is bringing everyone down. Perhaps it's a good time for you to just keep her at home and let her rest in her old age. From what the colonel has told me the woman practically raised him and he's thirty-five. So, I'd say after thirty-five years of devoted service she probably needs to rest. Tell her I said thank you for everything she's done but we won't be needing her anymore. Don't thank me but what you can do is send me to clean young wenches to begin in my kitchen right away."

"Yes ma'am. I will give her your message and send you a replacement this afternoon."

"Go on now. Git Andrew. I'm sure you have a lot of work that needs tendin'. And when you get a chance I want you go down to the lower forty and see how things are comin' along down there. I declare I cain't put no trust in that sorry ass Nicholson. I swear f' God he lazier than most a my niggras. I don't know why the colonel kept him around anyway. He's not worth his weight in salt."

"Miss Missy ma'am. Do you mind if I speak freely?"

"Ain't never stopped you before Andrew."

"Well, ma'am it appears to me that if you rotate the crops and have a certain group of niggras workin' a certain crop that they're particularly good at raisin' and you assign a niggra to be in charge of that particular field I expect he'd be rightly proud and you can bet they'd probably compete against each other to see whose field produces the most. In that way you can increase the yield from every crop and wouldn't have to

depend so much on just one crop to carry Three Winds. If cotton prices were to drop right now then we'd be in a hell mess since that's our only cash crop. But if you had cotton, tobacco, rice and other crops in different fields then you wouldn't have to rely so much on that one crop to sustain us. And if you rotated them you wouldn't have to worry about wearing out the soil."

"That's what Nicholson should have been suggestin'," missy replied not being able to grasp the entire concept but now understanding even more why her husband, the colonel held this niggra in such high esteem.

That done I knew I'd planted the seed. Now all I had to do was let it take root.

Mama was elated not to have to work for missy anymore and now spent her days teaching those too young to go to the fields to read and tending her garden. She seemed happier than any time since my father's death and I stayed close to home to keep an eye on her.

After checking in with mama I placed two of my closest confidantes in the big house to keep tabs on missy. Petunia had long ago grasped knowledge of the council and with the eventual idea of marriage planted in her mind I knew she could be trusted but the whipping she received at massa's orders before my father died made her a staunch believer in her own right. The fact that she had given birth to a beautiful baby boy some six years earlier only to have him taken from her and sold did little to endear her love for white folks or slavery making her one of the council's most loyal and trustworthy members.

Fiona, like most of us had her own horror stories. She was also a member of the council and these were the two I chose to place or better yet plant in the house with missy to keep surveillance. The fact that I slept with these two beautiful creatures had nothing at all to do with their placement although that very fact helped our cause perhaps more than any as women have a tendency to talk and recount some of the pleasures in life when idle or just chattering among themselves to pass the time.

A week or two later, missy pulled me aside to thank me for sending her two of the nicest niggra wenches she'd ever had the occasion to meet at which time I simply dropped my head and stared at the ground before me and simply muttered.

"Glad I could be of some help."

The two women were doing their jobs and with mama grooming them every evening they soon picked up the nuances of working for white folks and both seemed quite pleased that I had given them the opportunity to get out of the fields and out of that Mississippi sun. And each woman in her gratitude sought to repay me but I could foresee difficulties with this at the time and didn't need squabbling between the two in this rather delicate situation and so I politely declined. Still, and from what I understand they chattered away about my sexual prowess after dark and somehow missy got wind of it.

The colonel, Massa John had long since let it be known that he much preferred the thick, dark chocolate of the quarters and the milk chocolate mulattoes of New Orleans to

the pasty whiteness of his wife and so it was she that suggested separate sleeping quarters some years ago. But that wasn't to say that missy wasn't without needs and the more Fiona and Petunia spoke of their sexual encounters with me the more intrigued she became until a few days later she approached me alluding to the two girls conversation at which time I made no comment.

19

It was Saturday evening and as far as any of us knew all missy did in them days was sit and drink mint juleps and find something for us to do when she got bored with that until alas she would have Fiona or Petunia help her to bed where she would wile away the hours until sleep overcame her. And though I was but a slave I could never imagine such an existence. She had a library second to none and yet I'd yet to see her set foot in there let alone open a book which is perhaps why her life was so miserable. She simply did not avail herself of the gifts God set before her.

Occasionally she would entertain a guest but they were usually some friend of the colonel's just stopping by to pay their respects or to check on her to see how she was doing. Other than that her days were filled with the idea that she was running Three Winds which most of us knew was a falsehood since all of us had been there long before she showed up and as everyone knows a slaves life does not change very often.

She had little or no interests other than being a southern belle married to a plantation owner and as everyone knows that entails very little. So, when she considered the idea of testing the waters discreetly she approached me saying that she wanted me to do certain things to her and that if I whispered a word of it to anybody she would first

deny anything of the sort and then have me whipped before having me castrated and hung for defiling the honor of a white woman.

I was astounded and cursed both Fiona and Petunia and then I pled my case to Miss Missy's better judgment.

"Miss Missy may I speak freely?"

"Please do Andrew but you watch your tongue you hear? This happens to be a very sensitive subject to me."

"Yes ma'am." I answered. "And I am well aware of the repercussions should I not act accordingly. And Miss Missy ma'am if I do say so myself you are one beautiful white woman but I ain't never been with no white woman and I'm not sure I can perform like I do with a common colored girl."

"What's the difference Andrew?"

"You mean there ain't no difference between niggras and white folks Miss Missy ma'am?" I asked attempting o make her see the fallacy of her idiocy.

"I'm not discussing this any further with you Andrew. Tomorrow's Sunday and I've already told them gals that they don't have to work so there won't be anyone to interrupt us. Massa Nicolson has the night off and will be in Jackson until Monday. So, you see I've taken all the necessary precautions. I want you here as soon as the quarters are quiet."

I was quite taken back by this latest bit of news. A life or death situation should I be found out and with missy and her drinking I knew that any slip up on my part could lead to an early and painful death.

"Miss Missy ma'am as much as I would like to oblige you I cannot as the colonel and I grew up together and if for no other reason he sees me as his friend," I said sounding quite dejected that I wasn't able to help her in her time of need.

"What are you tellin' me niggra? Are you refusing a white woman's request? I am not asking you anything boy. I'm telling you you'll be here tonight. Do you understand me? Furthermore, you are no friend of my husband. You're no more than his slave; his property to do with what he so pleases. And just like my husband has the right to go down to the quarters or to New O'leans and get himself a nigga bitch to be his bed warmer then I too have the right to go to the quarters and get me a nigga bed warmer and you will warm my bed tonight. Is that clear nigga?" And with that she lifted her skirt and petticoats turned and bristled away.

I'm not sure how long I stood there. I thought of my father who would have doubled over in laughter if he had been there. I thought of going and grabbing Fiona and Petunia and whipping them myself and thought better of it. They would have thought the whole situation funny as well. And seeing no reasonable alternative I simply decided that I would not go

21

although I have to admit that I was curious to know what may have transpired. It didn't take me long to find out the outcome of my decision.

After a council meeting later that night that was cut short by the sound of slave catchers patrolling the road at regular intervals looking for runaways trying to get to Sherman's army we decided that we would reconvene on the fortnight.

Most of the slave patrollers were poor white trash of the worst sort. Rebuffed by the Confederate army for one reason or another they were often no better than thieves, robbers or ex-cons who looked for slaves, freedmen and almost any unwary suspect and sell them into bondage at the New Orleans market. Three or four of our own folks had disappeared in just such a manner over the last month or so and I thought it best that we curtail this new trade in human flesh but as we were not looking for an out-and-out confrontation so close to Sherman's army liberating us I saw no point in any of us spilling blood at this juncture when Sherman was willing to do it for us. We therefore crept back to our respective under the cover of darkness.

On my return, I was surprised to find one of my most trusted lieutenants, Jeremiah waiting for me at my cabin along with another young man of about twenty or so. As I approached I could sense something was terribly wrong but remained calm.

"Gentleman." I said greeting each with the respect so seldom granted us. "What is it that I can do for you at this late hour?"

"Miss Missy has sent us to fetch you sir. She wants us to bring you to the big house where we are to whip you," Jeremiah said the tears welling up in his eyes.

I could see the pain in his eyes. I knew he had little choice in the matter and I noticed that a crier had been sent to the quarters to wake up the rest of the niggras. They too were to be attendance to watch Three Winds favorite son being whipped for disobeying missy's directive.

"What's this all about?" Jeremiah asked the tears now flowing freely down the mammoth African's face.

"Nothing but a white woman trying to assert her authority. Nothing more. Nothing less," I explained trying to make light of the situation and ease Jeremiah's pain.

"They say Sherman's no more than twenty miles outside of Jackson. You can run. No need to get whipped on account of this drunk white bitch."

"You know my work is not done here Jeremiah. C'mon now. Let's get this over with. No need to go easy. I'll heal in time."

"You know what we need to do in this situation don't you Andrew? In a day or two Sherman will be here and no one will be the wiser."

"Trust me Jeremiah. This white woman in her drunken euphoria may be the key for all of us one day. Now let's not tarry these poor souls have to hit the fields early tomorrow."

Moments later the three men with Andrew Jackson walking proudly a step ahead of the other two approached the old oak. The crowd of two hundred or more slaves stood staring at the woman standing on the front porch.

Clearly intoxicated she yelled at the three men now standing no more than three feet in front of her.

"Ain't no nigga on Three Winds gonna deliberately disobey and if you even think about it this will happen to you as well. Now tie this belligerent nigga to the tree. I don't want his sorry ass to try and run."

But before she could finish her tirade Andrew turned and stepped proudly to the old oak where he lifted his arms letting his shirt fall to the ground before wrapping his arms around the tree.

"Let's do it Jeremiah. And spare nothing."

Jeremiah pulled the whip back and with all of his might let the whip lace Andrew's back biting deep into his flesh. The crowd of slaves turned as if on cue and stared at white woman on the porch.

"Whatcha y'all niggas lookin' at? If y'all don't turn around y'all gonna find yourselves up there next," but there was no response and they continued to stare at her hatred burning deep in each of their eyes.

"I can't wait til Lincoln does free y'all. Ya ain't nothin' but a bunch of wooly-haired good for nothin' coons." There was no response and after several more minutes she turned and walked into the mansion slamming the door behind her.

The blood which had been spurting a few inches at a time at regular intervals was soon stopped by some of the women there and a buckboard was soon brought over but Andrew who glanced back and saw missy peeking from an upstairs window refused the buckboard and any help. Bending over and picking up his shirt he glanced back exhibiting a big shiny pearly white smile before throwing one arm around Fiona and the other around Petunia and walking under his own accord back to the quarters.

Reaching the quarters and out of missy's sight he fell to his knees and then to his face. Jeremiah grabbed him like a sack of flour threw him across his shoulder and shouted at Fiona.

An hour or so later he resumed consciousness.

"Didn't know if you were gonna make it or not old man," Jeremiah grinned.

"There ain't nothing the white man can throw my way that I can't beat he said extending his hand towards his lieutenant.

"You did good man," he said smiling at Jeremiah. "First time in my life I've ever been whipped. I didn't know if I was going to make it or not."

"Well, no matter how many times it happens it never gets any easier. Trust me I know," he said letting his shirt drop from his back showing the scars of slavery. "So, are you going to share with us what made her wake up out of a drunken stupor and decide to whip you at midnight? You know missy is sleep every night at eight o'clock."

24

"Let that be my little secret but trust me that woman holds the key to our longevity but for now let me deal with that. Now no more questions. I had quite an eventful evening. Let me try and get some rest."

The next day proved formidable for me at best. Missy had little or nothing to say and seemed to be a vague shadow of herself at best passing in and out my day but hardly letting her presence be felt. Fiona was responsible for making her drinks and added a wee bit of laudanum to her mint julep at five o'clock. She was sound asleep by six and with Petunia posted outside of her bedroom door and Jeremiah posted outside the front gate I felt secure with lifting several boxes of books and sending them down to the quarters. I then had Fiona and Petunia switch places since Petunia was more proficient in her handwriting skills and forging Miss Missy's signature. Compiling a complete set of notes from Missy's stationery I sent my apprentice, young Buck into Jackson's General Store to secure some seed and some other supplies we needed down in the quarters.

The week went by rather quickly and with Fiona and Petunia taking turns nursing me my back was healing nicely. Missy now obviously cognizant of my position among

the slaves went easier on me that week but on Saturday she approached me again but this time her approach was more pleading than arrogant.

"Andrew I hope we will not have a repeat occurrence of what happened last week but I will be expecting you this evening. I hope your back will not deter you from coming."

I said nothing but understood that 'no' would not serve me well. When all was quiet in the quarters I made my way up to the big house and made my way around back to the servant's quarters where I found the door ajar.

"Is that you Andrew?"

"Yes, Miss Missy ma'am," I replied.

"Lock the door behind you and come up here."

I made my way up the winding staircase and to the sound of her voice. I had never seen her like this. She appeared younger than her years and vulnerable. This time it was she who dropped her head when she spoke.

"Andrew I apologize. Sometimes I let the drink get the best of me. I do so apologize. I guess I took out my own unhappiness on you. I am married to a man who feels no more towards me than he does his horse and his slaves. The truth is he pays more attention and gives more time to his nigga wenches than he does his own wife. He

doesn't love me," she said the tears flowing freely now. "It's a goddamn shame that I have to get one of his slaves to fuck me because he refuses to," she said before realizing she was confessing to a niggra. And then catching herself and realizing she was superior she turned her back to me lifted her petticoats revealing her naked ass and said.

"I want you to fuck me like you fuck them nigga wenches. I want you to fuck me like your life depended on it nigga and it just well might so you'd better pull out all the stops. I want you to rape this pretty white ass. If they don't hear me in the next county by morning I'll have the black whipped off you. Do you hear me? Now fuck me with that big, black nigga dick. Do you understand me nigga? I want you to fuck me good."

I didn't know if she was simply saying that to make it alright in her demented mind or if that's what she really wanted but I had no way of knowing and my back was only now starting to heal so I did my best to oblige. When she had come two or three times in a row she rolled over and smiled.

"Them gals wasn't lying. Now make love to me Andrew. Slow and gentle like…"

Again I did as I was told and she met my every move with one of her own. Grasping, clutching, biting and grabbing at anything she could get her hands onto including my back which was still raw. And all the while Miss Missy screamed calling

the heavens and earth but never calling me to do anything but give her more. I had nothing left now but she held on.

"Hold me Andrew. Just hold me."

I held her and realized that beneath me was no more than a troubled, scared little girl in need of love. There were no more niggas, no more massa slave innuendos there was just the scared little girl whose emotions were riding to close to the surface to make me feel comfortable. I was comfortable with the massa slave mentality. I had to be. I knew nothing else but she was frightening me now and all I wanted to do was get back to the quarters, to my cocoon of hatred for white folks and their hatred for me. But she held me.

"Andrew we have something good. Don't you think? I think this may turn out rather well for you and your people. You know there's a lot I can do for you and the rest of the niggras if you'd just let me."

"Yes ma'am."

"Oh my goodness. That was good," she said trying to swing her leg over the side of the bed and trying to get up then finding herself unable to. "Oh my. I think I pulled something," she said smiling. "Perhaps a bit too much after such a long absence. Do me a favor. Send one of the girls. I believe I'm going to need some assistance in the morning," she said still smiling. "But don't you mind me. I'll be good as new come Monday and then I'd like you to revisit that sweet spot you found so easily tonight. Do we have a deal?"

"Yes ma'am."

I got up and dressed quickly.

"Can I ask you something before you leave Andrew?"

"Yes ma'am."

"I want you to be honest with me."

"Yes ma'am."

"How was I in comparison to Fiona and Petunia?"

27

"You were fine ma'am."

"But was I as good?"

"You were as good if not better ma'am."

"Then why does the colonel prefer dark meat to me then?"

"Don't believe it has anything to do with your performance ma'am. I just believe it's what he grew up on."

"So, no matter what I do he will always prefer them?"

"I don't know ma'am. I believe that's something you may want to address with the colonel."

"Fuck the colonel!" Missy screamed. "I do believe I've found my own chocolate delicacy. I'll see you Monday night Andrew. And don't forget to send one of the girls up here in the morning."

"Yes, ma'am. Good night."

"Good night Andrew."

Walking back to the quarters that morning I thought long and hard about what had just transpired between Miss Missy and myself. It was a dangerous game in lieu of her state of mind. For me there was only one verdict should we be found out. For her it would mean certain banishment and exile even if she cried rape.

I examined the possibilities which were few. Miss Missy could be our greatest asset if I played my cards right. I at least had an avenue and though our conversation brief I came to know her vulnerabilities and was certain I could use these to our benefit but I also knew that her unpredictability—in large part due to her affinity for alcohol—could destroy us just as easily. It would be up to my girls Fiona and Petunia to bring her around slowly but did we have the time?

With Sherman so close—Vicksburg had just fallen—would there be time enough? We had already been able to procure a few hundred dollars due to her ineptness surrounding the books but this was minute on the threshold of three hundred or more slaves on Three Winds alone being freed with no foresight as to what the future would bring. These same concerns were had by most of the other council leaders when speaking of their own people.

I had already begun the diversity of raising multiple crops which would aid them in their eventual independency but the anger and animosity from southerners losing the war and the only culture they'd ever known made it hard to believe that we could be

autonomous in the beginning and market our crops to destitute slaves and white folks who had their farms and crops burned and found themselves equally as destitute.

Missy could serve as the perfect liaison but with the colonel returning her contribution certainly couldn't be relied upon. Unless…

It was at this moment that I knew the colonel could not return to Three Winds. By the time I reached the quarters I was certain of two things. If my plan was to be effective I had to continue letting Miss Missy have her way with the assumption that she was in charge. Her immense ego and arrogance would not allow her to believe anything to the contrary while at the same time securing certain inalienable rights to the slaves and thus enacting policies that would lead to us gaining self-sufficiency under her watchful eye. This all had to be her idea but I would certainly be there to lend a hand in the process. I was exhausted from the workout but more so drained mentally from the unscrupulous task of subtle coercion. I had to gain this white woman's undying trust and so I elicited Jeremiah's help who I knew was always up this time of night.

To my surprise Jeremiah was not in his cabin. Tired as I was—and I mean I was exhausted—I grabbed a seat on the ol' log he'd carved and fashioned into a chair and lit my pipe content to wait.

Not more than fifteen minutes later Jeremiah appeared from the edge of the woods. Jeremiah was never in a hurry to get anywhere and it took another few minutes to

cross the distance from the woods to his cabin. His face lit up when he saw me sitting there. We had been friends a long time but as of late we shared less and less time in each other's company. With all the work involved with the council, blacksmithing and looking in on mama I was already living on borrowed time and now with Miss Missy there left no time for old friends.

Jeremiah smiled when he saw me, pulled up another chair and took out his pipe. Handing him my pouch of tobacco I watched as he smiled.

"Just like old times," he muttered smiling.

"Just like old times," I said returning his smile and glad for the company of my old friend.

"What brings you here Andrew? I take it this is not just a social call."

"No," I said taking a long pull on my pipe and exhaling slowly before continuing. "I'm in need of your help and your advice," I said before explaining the situation with Miss Missy. And then I waited. Jeremiah had always been a man of deep thought and his insight was uncanny.

"So this is why she flogged you?" he surmised grinning from ear-to-ear before pausing again.

"If you had the ability—and I know that you do—you could turn her into perhaps our greatest asset. That would take time of course for you to cultivate a relationship and gain her trust. Even if Lincoln frees us little would likely change but if Lincoln frees us

the backlash against any niggras remaining in the South would make slavery look like a Sunday picnic. We had this very same discussion at the last council meeting."

"Was there a council meeting tonight?"

"No, boss."

"Oh, I just assumed that's where you were coming from?"

"No, that was a much needed little recreational retreat I went on over at the Handy Place."

"Oh," I said not daring to ask more. "Continue."

"In any case, and as you know the council members are very concerned with what and how to lead our people when the war's over. Many are—and I agree—under the impression that when the war ends between the states only then will the real war start for us niggra. We need to be able to compete from a business standpoint so that we are able not only to grow our crops but to be able to sell 'em and compete and receive fair compensation. That's why it's so important for us to be able to read."

"You're absolutely right."

"We need the money to buy the seed and tools to sell and sustain us and we need weapons to ward off the returning troops who have not given up the idea of enslaving us.

Miss Missy can be a very important instrument in getting us those things. And land as well."

"And land as well," I agreed.

"You do realize she's crazy don't you?"

"As a Betsy bug."

"And you do know if you two are found out she will say you raped her? "I do."

"Then you know the risks. Knowing all that you must ask yourself if it's worth it? I cannot answer that for you."

"I don't think at this point I have a choice. It's either commit to her insanity and try to turn her into a sympathetic ear or take another whipping from you," I said smiling.

Jeremiah dropped his head in shame.

"I am so sorry Andrew."

"No need to apologize my friend. We know where the real culprit lies and with your help we can have her eating out of our hands in little or no time," I said smiling. I had a plan.

The patrollers were getting worse and many had changed their emphasis from catching runaways to out-and-out kidnapping and I insisted on us making sure that if we were on the fringes of Three Winds or on the roads that we made sure that we were never alone and stayed in groups as patrollers were as a lot highwaymen, robbers and thieves who had now seen the war as an opportunity to make a living out of human trafficking.

And with that said a fourteen year old boy had just this morning gone missing. His mother had awakened to fix him a lunch to go on a fishing adventure with two or three of his friends. The other boys came rushing back within minutes to say how two white men had tried to snatch them up down by the creek. They had escaped but he had fallen and the men had snatched him. I sent for Jeremiah, Josiah and Fiona and grabbed one of the colonel's rifle's Petunia had lifted for me when Miss Missy was in one of her drunken stupors and had the boys lead me to the creek.

Jeremiah, Josiah and Fiona met me a few minutes later. Josiah a white sharecropper of about twenty three was sympathetic to our cause and acted as a front man for our cause on several occasions. He had gained our respect in the last year or so going on a few of the council's expeditions but that was not to say he was a member or would ever be. Nevertheless he shared in the spoils of many of our capers as an active and willing participant.

The boys were then dismissed after pointing the way the patrollers had gone. They too were on foot and we knew that if we made haste we would surely overtake them. Half an hour later we caught sight of the two

32

men which had actually grown to three and the string of six or seven slaves they now had in their custody. I gave the colonel's rifle to Josiah. We had reenacted this situation many times before and were well rehearsed each knowing our role.

Approaching the slaves and looking them over the first one of us to recognize the boy would yell out. It was Fiona who spotted him first.

""Lord Jesus here's my baby!" Fiona shouted out. "Oh massa they done stole baby."

"Now, now ain't nobody done stole yo baby. Calm down gal," Josiah said. "Who is you to be accusin' some white men of stealin'? You best know yo'place nigga."

Fiona moved back from the boy dropping her head apologetically knowing she had spoken out of turn.

Josiah then turned back to the patrollers.

"I am sorry gentlemen for this niggas outburst but if you don't mind me askin'," he said pausin' to get a chaw of tobacco from his pouch and forcing it into his mouth.

"Again I apologize but if you would be so kind could you please tell me how you come across this here nigga?"

"Well, I could if you'd first tell me who the hell you are?"

"Name's Josiah Handley and I'm the ovaseer of the Three Winds Plantation and it has come to our attention that there are patrollers who may have mistakenly picked up one of our niggras as a runaway. I'm here to retrieve him my good man."

"Looks like the description of a runaway to me."

"Perhaps you'd like to come over here outta earshot for a chat," Josiah said to the patroller as he reached in his jacket pocket for his flask. Seeing the flask the man joined Josiah on a log not far away.

"Seems to me none of the niggras you got is runaways. I recognize a couple of them niggras from the O'Reilly Place where I used to be ovaseer. And you know it just don't seem likely that any slave's gonna run with Sherman a day North," Josiah said sipping from the flask and then passing it to the patroller who gladly accepted it. "In fact and to be honest with you I don't think there's a niggra that you have chained up that's a runaway. I think that you're simply po' white trash trying to make a few dollars at a time

a niggra ain't gonna fetch you much wit' Lincoln getting' ready to free 'em. But y'all too dumb to realize that."

You could see anger growing in the man's eyes as he took another swig from the flask but said nothing as Josiah shifted the rifle from his left hand to his right.

"If you had any brains you'd let these po' wretched souls go and rob something that can make you some real money."

"Keep talkin'" the man said passing the bottle back to Josiah.

"Listen friend. Three River Plantation is the one of the largest counties around and ain't nobody around. The colonel's gone off to fight the Yanks and ain't nobody around to guard that house after dark. Miss Missy is the only one around after dark. It's a piece of cake and Missy's jewelry is worth ten times what these here niggas would bring if slavery was in its prime. You hit it once and you'll be set for life. Just give me a lil somethin' for the tip. I've thought about it once or twice but being that I work there I could never get away with it but being that they ain't never seen you before it would be a cakewalk."

"And you say this Missy is the only one stayin' there?"

"The only one but I don't want her hurt. Missy's a good woman. Drinks a might too much but she's a good woman."

"And what time does she usually go to bed?"

34

"Well, I can have this wench give her a shot of laudanum with her tea and guarantee she be asleep by seven thirty. If you hi I at eight o'clock sharp you should be out of there by nine o'clock at the latest."

"You can meet me at O'Bannion's Pub on the south fork right before you hit Jackson and we can divvy up the take and I can get you set up to hit O'Reillys. I know that place like the back of my hand too."

The men stood and shook hands.

"Now let me take these sorry wretches back to their rightful owners," Josiah said before spitting and taking another long swallow from the flask.

"Unchain them niggas," the man said to his second in charge.

One of the slaves, a woman in her middle age ran up to me.

"You can't fool me. That white man might have been doin' the talkin' but I know who it was that was runnin' things. I don't know your name but I seen you and I heared about you. I want to thank you for myself and for my babies who almost ain't had no mama.

I'm a good Christian woman but I think the good Lord would forgive me in this case so if there's anything I can do to thank you. Anything at all…," she said makin' no

bones about what was available. I declined hugged the woman and then caught up with Josiah.

"How did it go?"

"Everything is right as rain. They'll be there tomorrow. We can finish the job then," Josiah said.

"You did well Josiah. You'll be rewarded."

"In God's eyes I already am," he replied.

According to Petunia Miss Missy was fit to be tied when we returned. And although it was Sunday and our one day of rest I knew where missy was concerned that could easily be changed.

"I'm not sure I even want to know."

"Told me to go fetch you. When I told her you won't nowhere to be found she had a hissy fit. I don't know what you done done to that woman but if she could have found you Lord knows what she would have done to you this time."

"Do you know what she wanted?"

"Now you know miss high and mighty and sharin' nothin' with a common niggra wench."

"Thought you may have overhead something."

"How am I going to overhear somethin'? It ain't like she got someone to talk to. T'aint nobody there but me and her. I don't know how she stays up in that big ol' house all alone. It's downright spooky if you ast me. Put some laudanum in her tea to quiet her down some but that ain't even have no effect. When I left she was still hollerin' and screamin'. And she got a bad limp this mornin'. When I ast her if she fell or pulled a muscle she cussed me out so bad I just shut my mouth and didn't ast her about nothin' after that. Po' woman cain't hardly walk. I think she may won't you to fashion her some crutches. Anyway, she told me to go find you and don't come back without you. You know she don't come down to the quarters on a good day and bein' that she cain't walk you ain't got nothin' to worry about. I am curious to know what happened to her. She screamed all night last night did you hear her?"

"Can't say that I did. C'mon. Let's go see what's wrong. If not they'll be hell to pay and my back's still not healed yet."

Petunia climbed the winding staircase to Missy's bedroom and knocked on the bedroom door.

"Miss Missy it's me."

36

"Come here gal and help me out this bed. I take it you found him?"

"Yes, ma'm. He's outside on the front porch."

"Well, come on girl. Don't tarry. And I'm gonna need you to fix me a little something to ease some of this here pain. A pitcher of Mint Juleps will do fine. Bring it out to the front porch."

"Yes ma'am."

Missy's face took on a lighter, friendlier glow upon seeing Andrew standing there.

"Mornin' ma'am."

"Morning Andrew. "

"Petunia tells me you want to see me."

"Yes. Gal where is that drink?"

"I is coming Miss Missy," Petunia said smiling at me.

"Well, you are certainly taking your sweet ass time about it. I swear fo' God I ain't never seen a nigga so goddamn slow."

"Well, you ast me to add a lil' somethin' to ease the pain missy and the doctor say that if I don't measure just the quite dose of laudanum it could prove lethal," Petunia said trying to sound serious and just waiting for the day Andrew would give her the word to poison this ol' evil white woman.

"Is you sassing me again gal. I don't know why I continue to put up with you and your mouth gal but you keep on. One day I'm going to have all that pretty, black whipped off of you Petunia. Now help me out to the porch so I can have a word with Andrew." "Yes ma'am," Petunia said helping Missy out to the porch and onto the swing.

"Will there be anything else ma'am?"

"No, Petunia. If there is I'll be sure to call you."

"I know you will ma'am," Petunia said sarcastically as she walked away.

Ignoring her Missy turned her attention to Andrew.

"I suppose you're wondering why I had Petunia summon you," she said taking a long swig of the Mint Julep on the table in front of her."

"The thought did occur to me ma'am," I replied cautiously.

"Well I was lying in bed thinking that with the Yankee soldiers close by and with the colonel being away I could use someone close at hand."

"And you're saying that to say what ma'am?"

"I was just thinking that instead of me having to have someone summon you whenever I need you that it would just be more convenient if you built a cabin right here in back of the Magnolia House."

I suppose it was food for thought but I was having a hard digesting missy's latest proposal.

"Pardon me ma'am but don't you think that would raise suspicions among both niggras and white folks ma'am and what would the colonel ink about a niggra living so close to his wife ma'am?"

I didn't call you up here for a discussion or your opinion Andrew. I want you to start building tomorrow. I want you to draw up plans for your cabin and then pick for or five of our best niggras and I want you to commence building tomorrow. Leave room for a garden if you like and make it so you're comfortable. I want the world to see how Three Winds treats its prime niggras. And not that I owe you any explanation nigga but since you asked, I will tell you that I don't give a goddamn what niggras conjure up in their tiny lil minds or what white folks think either. As far as the colonel's concerned I have a pretty good idea that the colonel will not be returning to Three Winds after the war. "Has something happened to the colonel ma'am?" I asked a bit surprised to hear this latest news.

38

"Let's just deal with you drawing up the plans tonight. Now if you go into the library you'll find paper and charcoal. I want to see the plans first thing in the morning Andrew," and with that Miss Missy hobbled back into Magnolia House under her own power and with the help of one Mint Julep laced with laudanum.

Again I walked back to the quarters perplexed. There was really no need for me to be housed next to the Magnolia House other than to cater to her carnal desires without having to continually send or look for me.

Still, this move would not allow me the freedom to address folks concerns in the quarters my council duties and again I had no choice and upon returning I contracted five or six of the finest carpenters in the quarters and commissioned these men along with Jeremiah and Josiah to accompany me and begin construction that evening.

It was perfect. That evening after having drawn the plans for the cabin I had Petunia summon Missy to come and view the plans. She was walking a little better now with less of a limp and was excited that I'd had the wherewithal and seemed as excited as she was about moving so close to her.

"Oh, Andrew it's simply marvelous. It is truly grand! And you say you want to begin construction now? Well, by all means get started. I'll have Petunia fix y'all boys some lemonade," she said looking in Petunia's direction. "And fix me a lil pick me up as well."

I glanced at Petunia on cue and she knew that I needed Missy awake which meant no laudanum.

"Miss Missy ma'am I was wondering if I could borrow one of the colonel's rifles so I could do a little hunting in the morning? "Sure, Andrew. I'll give Petunia the key to the colonel's gun case and she'll show you to them. "And I knew I could have asked for anything at this point but there would be time for that later. Right now one or two rifles and a shotgun would suffice.

Not long after Missy came out to the clearing and watched our initial clearing of the land which seemed to fascinate her before retiring into the house for the evening. Not long after she was gone we set up at five o ten intervals in the tree line out-of-sight and waited. Around eight when the sun had gone down Fiona approached me under the shadows of darkness.

"Jeremiah said he saw three riders approaching. They tied their horses down the road a ways but inside of Three Winds and are headed towards Magnolia."

"Good! Good! Tell everyone to let them enter the house and then join me here."

Fiona left quietly.

Moments later I watched as the ringleader of the patrollers jimmied the back door and went into the house. I then waited a moment or two until I heard Missy scream. We didn't want it to seem like we were lying in wait or were in any way connected so we took our sweet time about going in. When we finally did go in Missy scream seemed more subtle which I knew was quite unlikely Missy who I'd heard scream uninterrupted for four o five hours straight just a day or so ago. Rushing up the stairs and into her boudoir I understood why as missy had been stripped then bound and gagged, her ankles tied to the bedposts. The ringleader already has his pants down and his two cohorts held missy's arms outstretched.

"Put your hands up gentlemen," I said leveling the shotgun at all of them. They knew that at such close range I could have sprayed all of them with one blast. Fiona rushed over grabbing the afghan at the end of the bed to cover missy's naked genitals. Lifting their hands warily the ringleader smiled and looked at me.

"Say boy. It looks like you got me but you could at least me finish this sweet white piece of meat." I looked at missy who was by now quite terror stricken. Less than a week ago she had had me raped and I let these thoughts stir around in her mind for a minute before I turned to Jeremiah.

"Jeremiah would you please have these gentlemen tied up and taken away from here."

Only Fiona was left now. She quickly untied the panic stricken woman and took the gag from Missy's mouth.

"Are you okay ma'am?" Fiona asked.

"Yes, I'm okay Fiona. Thank you so much," she said before bursting into tears.

"Are you sure ma'am?"

"Yes, Fiona. You can go now."

I was the only one left and as soon as Fiona closed the door missy stood and walked toward me before bury her head in my shoulder. I wrapped my arms in an attempt to console her. Clearly shaken she sobbed and I could feel her tiny shoulders heave beneath the weight of what had just transpired. When she finally composed she looked up at me.

"Andrew those men were going to rape me," she said staring into my eyes as if they held the answer. I wanted to say, Isn't that why you want me to build this cabin so you could rape me whenever you have the notion but thought better of it knowing my position.

"I'm so glad you were near. Lord must have been smiling on me having you here at my time of need. I could have been killed."

"Yes, you very could have. I'll send Petunia and Fiona up to stay with you tonight ma'am," I said turning to leave.

"I owe you so much Andrew but please don't send them. I want you to stay with me tonight. You don't have to do anything Andrew. I just don't want to be alone tonight."

"Are you sure ma'am?"

"Yes, Andrew I am sure."

I laid down next to this white woman who snuggled up under me. And after kissing me and attempting to mount me found that she was too swollen and too sore for intercourse.

"It's a funny thing," she said after making several failed attempts. "That as you grow older your mind may crave and desire but your body simply won't allow you to follow through?"

"I'm not sure that that's age ma'am. After a night like last night anyone would be able to repeat a performance like that."

"Perhaps you're right Andrew," she said propping herself up on my chest and staring deep into eyes. "Would you be so kind as to run downstairs and get me something cold to drink and would you put a dash of feel better in it so we can try once more. I owe you so much I want to thank you in some way tonight and I know your people never grow tired of pussy and what can be better than some white pussy to a niggra slave? Now hurry. You know it's gonna take a minute for the medicine and I'm oh so very tired Andrew. I just want to say thank you in a way I know you'll appreciate."

I could hear my pappy's words as I mixed the drink and had to stop myself for pouring her a lethal dose of laudanum. Why did white folks always think they knew what was best for a niggra? Why did they walk around with this air of superiority and have it fixed in their minds that we were unthinking, unfeeling and unknowing? It was this arrogance and air of superiority which would be their eventual undoing. I had to stop from pouring the laudanum. I stood there and watched my hand shake. I thought about how important Missy could prove to be.

She'd already alluded to the fact that the colonel would not be returning from the war. That in itself was worth a pass. I really had no idea how she planned on making that come to fruition. The colonel was no journey highwayman and with the power and holdings he wielded throughout the state his untimely demise would certainly warrant a

full investigation unless it was accepted by his wife. And the benefits she was already providing were immeasurable with her accepting my proposals for Three Winds with no ultimatums other than I bed her down on her request. And although it went against my very constitution it was but a cheap price to pay for the fulfillment of my people. Mama was already in a better position than she'd ever been since her arrival here. And folks who were starving not more than a year ago were now well fed and prospering.

"Andrew. Andrew what is taking you so long?"

Still tempted I capped the bottle of laudanum then reopened it and poured a little more. There were things I still had to do once she was asleep.

"Sorry, ma'am. I had a hard time finding everything."

"I want you to take some time either today or tomorrow acclimating yourself with Magnolia," she said drinking much of the glass in one fell swoop. "Let's talk while I'm waiting for this to affect Andrew."

"What do you want to talk about ma'am?" I said afraid of what was going to come from her mouth now.

"First, of all I'd prefer if you'd forget the formalities when you're in my bed. I want you to call me Missy not Miss Missy or ma'am. Do you understand?"

"Yes, ma'm."

"Okay, well I see that's going to take some time. In the meantime, let me ask you something Andrew. The Confederacy has lost the war."

"Is that right ma'am. Has the South lost the war?"

"Don't play dumb with me Andrew. You're one of the brightest people I know so don't go playin' that dumb, I don't know nothin', po' shufflin' niggra role with me. If we're to be intimate I deserve more than that," she said sippin' the rest of the drink and resting her chin on my chest.

"I'm not sure I can do that ma'am."

43

"And why may I ask can't you. Here I am lying next to you with my body naked and exposed. Something I've only done with my husband and you're telling me you can't talk to me."

"My speaking freely could have me whipped and killed ma'am."

"Are you telling me that you have so much hatred towards the whites that if you told me how you truly felt you fear it would or possibly could to me having you whipped or killed?"

"I don't know ma'am but don't you think that's too high a price to pay for me to wax eloquent."

"Yes, I suppose it is. And since I have finally found some happiness even if it's only in the bed then I certainly don't want to disrupt that. I guess for now this will have to suffice. Maybe over time we can hope to become better acquainted as friends. Do you think that's possible Andrew?"

"I would like to think so."

"You know I've noticed how well you are received and respected by the niggras on Three Winds. They look to you for direction. So let me ask you this."

"Yes."

"When the war ends and President Lincoln frees the slaves will you and the other niggras remain on here at Three Winds?"

"That depends."

"I'm listening."

"There is not a slave on Three Winds that chooses to be a slave. However, this is the only home any of us has ever known. But given our freedom there is not a slave here that wouldn't take the chance at starting all over and owning a piece of land that he can call his own and being paid for his labor."

"So, what you're telling me is that when Lincoln frees the slaves they'll be a mass exodus?"

"They're already is ma'am. They're saying Sherman has almost as many runaway slaves attached to his army as he has troops."

"Oh my Lord! Is it that bad? So who will run and manage Three Winds Andrew?"

"I believe that's up to you and the colonel ma'am."

"There is no colonel. It's just me now Andrew."

"I been meaning to ask you about that ma'am. You keep referring to the fact that the colonel will not be returning from the war but you never once said what has happened to my friend the colonel."

"You and I both know that the colonel has never really been a friend of yours Andrew and I don't think that's any of your business."

"And you say you want to cultivate a friendship or is it that you just want me to divulge things to you without you having to do the same"

"Touché," she said smiling. "Okay if you must know I've arranged so that the colonel will not make it home from the war."

"You mean you aim to have him killed?"

"The colonel is no husband. He's a terrible businessman and since his daddy died Thee Winds has been in arrears. He serves absolutely no purpose and he's abusive. He has to be put down."

I said nothing.

"So, what is it that would keep the niggras from leaving Three Winds when President Lincoln emancipates them?"

"Well, if you can entertain the fact that these are men with families to support then you have to realize that the first thing a man wants is his own. He wants his own land, his own crops so he can provide for his family. Those two things alone could be very persuasive in keeping most of the

45

niggras on Three Winds and it would have to be done now before Lincoln frees them. If it's done after he frees them it will only look like a last ditch effort to keep them in bondage and to a people who have been beaten and lied to your word wouldn't amount to a hill of beans. If I were you I would seize the opportunity to do it now. Tomorrow. By now the word has spread throughout the quarters that three white men tried to rob and rape the mistress of Magnolia. And her colored slaves fought off these white men. In her appreciation she is granting each of her adult slaves five to ten acres in appreciation as long as they stay on and work the land. That would still leave you with close to four hundred acres. And that's quite a tidy sum of land and with them working it could be very profitable, especially with the right man running it and much me profitable than it is right now."

Missy smiled.

"If I didn't know any better I'd say that you'd already given this considerable thought."

"I have. Those white men that came here tonight were a blessing of sorts."

Missy was puzzled.

"Don't you see they gave you good cause to make the announcement.

Otherwise niggras would only look at the gesture with skepticism and cynicism and ask why you were being so generous after treating them with cruelty and utter disdain up 'til now."

"I do see your point. Thank you Andrew. I'll have to take that into consideration. Now give me cause to thank you again," she said kissing me deeply and passionately.

"It's a sad world that states who you can and can't love."

"Love?" I said looking puzzled.

"No, silly the verb. As in I am going to love you now with unbridled passion," she said smiling. The alcohol and laudanum obviously in full affect as she grimaced in pain as she eased down on me.

Once she had taken me deeply inside of her she stopped.

"Of course it's not totally inconceivable that if we can learn to be friends we can so too learn to be in love."

"I may have to tend to agree with you in one aspect. This world of massa and slave won't ever allow that to happen."

"Oh, Andrew you are ever the pessimist. You can look through life like you're looking at a glass. You either see it as being half empty or half full. Already I see myself as being physically in love with you and now feel like I may be falling in love with you."

"Don't say that ma'am. That would surely be the death of both of us."

"Let me worry about that Andrew," she said as she began to ride him in earnest.

When missy awoke the next morning she found Andrew long gone and the sound of carpenters hard at work. Looking out the window she was surprised to see the frame of the cabin already up. It was minute in comparison to Magnolia but three times the size of any slave quarters with two stories. She certainly hadn't seen that in the plans.

Dressing quickly she called from the top of the staircase.

"Fiona, Petunia!"

Both girls came scurrying.

"Ma'am," they both said in unison.

"Have you seen Andrew?"

"I do believe you told him he could go hunting this morning ma'am," Fiona said

"You're right. I did. Well, you tell him I want to see him just as soon as he gets back. You wouldn't likely know where he goes hunting?"

"Yes, ma'am. He always goes right over there on Cedar Bluff ma'am," Petunia volunteered.

"Well, would you run over there and fetch him for me right quick?"

"No ma'am."

"Excuse me wench."

"No disrespect ma'am but that's like committin' suicide. Last night time I went to hunt him down he thought I was a white toed deer and damn near shot my head off. Not only that the patrollers is all over the place lookin' for runaways," Petunia said waiting to feel the wrath of Miss Missy's foul mouth or worse. But to both Fiona and Petunia's surprise there was no foul mouthed language to follow.

"Okay Petunia just tell him I'd like to see him when he returns."

Both women looked at each other in disbelief and turned to walk in the kitchen when they were called back.

"Why are both of you up here on a Sunday morning?"

"T'ain't just us ma'am. Every niggra on the place out front on account of Andrew saying that you might have something to tell us that gonna change all our lives."

"Oh, he said that did he?" Missy said before smiling a broad grin and walking away.

"You sure y'all got there in time last night and them white men ain't poke her once or twice before you saved her puny ass?"

"I'm sure. But that's not to say that someone ain't hit it after I left," Fiona said grinning.

"And who was there after you left?"

"Andrew."

Both women fell out.

"No wonder she lookin' for him," Petunia said still laughing.

"That's why she fixin' to do somethin' nice for us niggras. He hit it again and we may all be movin' up to Magnolia."

"If he works that thing like he used t work mine she may trade Magnolia for a one room dirt floor cabin in the quarters," Petunia said falling out on the kitchen table.

"Ladies did I miss the joke?"

"Ahh, no ma'am, Fiona whispered.

I returned at a little after noon only to find almost all of the three or so niggra slaves spread out around the big house with Miss Missy sitting in her customary position on the porch in front reading something or another.

She seemed quite content and at peace which was in and of itself very unusual but there she was reading not screaming and shouting obscenities telling niggras to fetch this and fetch that. No, she just sat there while the children ran and jumped and wrestled laughing and cried and I thought by God there may still be hope.

When she saw me I was sure that all that was to come to an end but instead she rose from the porch swing.

"Andrew may I speak to please," she said smiling slightly.

Moving closer her smile disappeared.

"Would you mind telling me why all of these people are gathered here today?"

"I'm sorry but I was under the impression that you were interested in keeping Tree Winds intact."

"I told you I would think about it."

"Missy not to be rude or disrespectful but the time to act is now. If you don't these people are going to walk away when Sherman comes through or Lincoln frees them. Three Winds cannot pay a labor force of three hundred people. If you don't make them this offer today you're apt to lose them all by the end of the week."

"Are you threatening me Andrew?"

"No. I'm just telling you the truth ma'am. It's entirely up to you how you proceed with it."

"Move out of my way Andrew. I'll deal with you later," she said pushing him aside.

Jeremiah who was never far from Andrew's side was then summoned by Missy.

"Call them to order Jeremiah."

"Okay y'all listen up! Miss Missy has an important message to make that will affect all a y'all."

Missy stood up and walked to the edge of the porch.

"As most of y'all are aware of it looks like the war is coming to an end. It's a sad day for both the North and the South. With all the blood that's been spilled I don't think there's a clear winner. Both sides have lost thousands of good men. Men that believed that their cause was right and just. Many of you niggras think that you are the ultimate winners but you also have a dilemma to face. Freedom will allow you to go as you please. But my question is where will you go? For many of you this is the only home you know. And I am not forcing you off of Three Winds. What I am suggesting is that

you stay on not as slaves but as land owners. I need people to wok the lands and you need someplace to live. What I propose is that you work the land for five years and I will give each of you five acres. For those of you that want more land—say ten acres—I want ten years. That's an acre for every year that you commit to working. Think it over. You have 'til sunset to come up and put your mark on this piece of paper. At sunset I will take it in to Jackson and go before the judge and the land office and make it all official. When I return those of you who choose to sign up will be given a deed to your land.

For those of you who choose to leave Three Winds and venture out on your own the colonel and I thank you for your time and your servitude."

There was a quiet hush and then a low murmuring as families turned trying to understand what Missy had just said. No. There was no way Missy was going to sell off three winds. No. It had to be a ploy on this white woman's part when Jeremiah called them to order again.

"It is four thirty now. Go home and eat dinner. Talk about it amongst yourselves and see what best fits your needs. I know there are a lot of questions so we will meet in the lower forty and discuss it further. I hope you all will attend."

"Andrew would you take a walk around to the back with me please?"

I would have walked with her anywhere she asked at this point. It was the first time in my life I had seen a plantation owner concede anything more than a ham at Christmas time to his slaves. But something as valuable as land was a chance, an opportunity for a new life. It was a chance for a man, a niggra, a colored man, a former slave to stand tall and say this is mine. It meant ownership and a chance to be independent and self-sufficient. And in some way I played a part in all of this. Oh, how proud m'pappy would have been of me.

"Thank you ma'am. You've made a lot of very worried people very happy today," I said with frank sincereness.

51

"That's all well and good Andrew and I'm happy for your people but don't you ever put me on the spot like that again," she said in a vain attempt to let me know she was still in charge of Three Winds but everyone else knew who was really running and her having to wait to confer with me before addressing us was confirmation. Still, for all of intensive purposes it was her signature that was recognized when anything was to be appropriated or considered legal and binding and not mine.

"My next bit of concern is this monstrosity you are attempting to build here."

"Ma'am?"

"I looked over your plans and what started out as a simple one room cabin has now turned into a two story home that looks to rival Magnolia."

"Oh no, ma'am this is just a cottage in comparison to grand ol' Magnolia house with all its Victorian Style and grandeur."

"That very well may be. But it's a mansion when compared to a typical slave quarters."

"But ma'am I wasn't building this for a slave but a free man. And you were so insistent on showing the world how you treat your good niggras that I tried to give the best reflection of you and your charitable nature that I could."

"I think you've grown too big for your own good Andrew," she said dismissing my rhetoric.

I said nothing but smiled aware for the first time that she was now weak and susceptible to change as long as it didn't disturb her new found happiness. Still, her insatiable needs needed to be dealt with most tenderly.

"Ma'am."

"Yes, Andrew."

"I killed two beautiful ducks this morning. Fiona fixes a wonderful duck with and orange marmalade sauce. I was hoping that you would sit with me for dinner and perhaps a drink or two and perhaps we could make an evening of it on our way to cultivating our newfound friendship."

Missy smiled but paused before responding to my query.

"You're quite the charmer Andrew. But first I believe you have a meeting with a group of new landowners. I believe they're gonna need some reassurance that the evil white landowner is not going to try and enslave them again. Wouldn't want t be in your shoes?"

I smiled.

"And tell them that they better make up their minds quickly before the evil white devil woman changes her mind."

"I don't think you would do that."

"I was coerced against my will."

"I think you enjoy being coerced ma'am."

"Perhaps. And I know how you feel about your people. There may be some more coercion needed right up until I sign those deeds. Then we'll look at just what other concessions need to be made. A parcel of land is just a parcel of land with no seed, livestock or tools to work it. Wouldn't you agree Andrew?"

"I think this is a conversation best served over a glass of spirits."

"Shall we say six o'clock?"

"Seven would be even better."

"Seven it is then and bring a riding crop."

"Will do ma'am."

I left feeling a sense of renewed hope. She understood the trade off and to her it was a fair trade. Her needs were being fulfilled and in lieu of that she would make the necessary concessions. What I was curious to know and it would ultimately dictate her fate was if she had any compassion, any guilt or were her actions purely out of her own selfish desires and need for satisfaction.

But for now I had other concerns as the O'Reilly Plantation one of the chief supporters of the Confederate War effort were still not letting up on their slaves and had made it clear that slavery was and always would remain a staple even if secession failed.

And in all the years I've known ol' Ben never have I seen him so distraught. The O'Reilly's were no more than a group of poor Irish trash who arrived here due to a famine in Ireland and became perhaps the harshest critic of the niggra. Whippings and hangings inevitable were commonplace on the O'Reilly Place and conditions were said to be worse than on most plantations. Now faced with the almost inevitable idea of slavery ending they had gone to extreme measures to make sure that there were no runaways and that the idea of slave and master remained intact.

Ol' Ben was at his wits ends. Always one of the cooler heads he was up in arms and I knew an immediate solution was desperately needed.

"Things ain't never been whatcha might call good over there but with Sherman closing in and all this talk about freeing the slaves O'Reilly and his boys done got outright mean. You look the wrong way and they liable to hang you up. Whipped my daughter to within an inch of her life because she fought the youngest O'Reilly boy when he tried to have his way with her. He told m'baby that 'wasn't no nigga heifer gonna go into no freedom a virgin.' That's what he told m'baby and she ain't but twelve. Them fools done got downright vicious over the sound of freedom. Just yesterday they hung ol' Pete 'cause they say he wasn't movin' fast enough. I knowed ol' Pete all my life. The man was damn near eighty years old. How fast can you expect an eighty year old to move?" Ben said his eyes welling with tears.

"I tell you and everyone here knows that I ain't never been one for violence 'ceptin' in extreme cases but this here's an extreme case. Them

O'Reilly's is the devil himself. That's the third niggra they done hung this week." He said the tears now flowing freely.

"This thing at the O'Reilly place has gone on for far too long. They've been well documented as being some of the worst owners in the county ever since I can remember. I do believe it's time for ol' man Reilly and his boys to pay to the piper. Let me see a show of hands of all those in favor."

Ol' Ben who seldom if ever voted for violence was the first hand up.

"Only thing left to decide on is when. I vote next Saturday after them boys get all likkered up. All in favor…"

Ol' Ben interrupted.

"Can't wait that long Andrew. This ain't no ordinary case. We may lose four or five niggras by next Saturday. It must be done today! Now!"

I knew that anytime Ben was this adamant things were in a bad way so I agreed even though I hated to move in such a hurried fashion. Proper planning and preparation was essential in planning a successful undertaking and rushed plans often led to failure but sensing the gravity of Ben's predicament I planned the raid for the following night.

On the way back from the council meeting Jeremiah, Fiona and I walked a good mile in silence until Fiona broke the tranquility with a thought that I am sure was on everyone's mind.

"You know after today with us all gaining our own piece of land and the war being so close to the end and us gaining our freedom I hate to think of us putting our lives on the line now," she said echoing my sentiments exactly.

"Same thing I was thinking back there when ol' Ben was talking," Jeremiah said. "But you know the war is only over for the white boys. I have a feeling the real war is just beginning for the niggra. How we doing as far as you conscripting some rifles from Missy, Andrew?"

55

"I've been given that a lot of thought Jeremiah and for the life of me I can't figure out an angle on how to get her to do that."

"That's a tough one Jeremiah," Fiona answered. "No matter how tight Andrew gets with that white woman and no matter how much she trusts him that's a tough call for her to arm the very people she had whipped and beaten. I would think twice about ding that iffen I was in her shoes. A niggra is liable to get a rifle and no sooner than he gets it loaded the first person he would think about usin' it on would be the person that had him whipped last week."

"And adding a rifle and shotgun to every order that goes in to the general store is only going to raise suspicions. Right now we've got a total of twenty new rifles and eight shotguns. Hardly enough to arm all of us or ward off attacks. The best we can do at this point is conduct a small raid here and there but no more than that."

"Ain't we got no one in the general store that we can get to order an extra rifle or revolver every time Jones places his order?"

"Only Calvin and he can't read or write. Besides ol' man Jones does all his ordering and figgerin' himself. I don't think he even allows Mrs. Jones near his books," Jeremiah said.

"He is one tight fisted ol' boy ain't he?" Fiona countered.

"Yeah, and he ain't never been sympathetic to our cause that's why I had to stop throwing in a rifle or two with our orders. He liable to ride out here to see Missy and ask what all the rifles is for but what I will do the when the time is right is speak with Missy about ordering some fifty or sixty rifles so we can go hunting but first I'll let her get them deeds notarized. The word about her donating land to her niggras should spread like wildflower and then it won't come as much of a shock to Jones and others like him. Chances are they'll call her down font about arming a buncha niggras but she's a tough ol' bird and iffen she thinks we loyal to her it won't bother her too much. She's already bought in to the fact that by deedin' the niggras the land is the onliest way she can keep Three Winds."

"I don't know why that should be so hard to swallow. That's the truth."

"It is but that's revolutionary thinking. Most southerners believe that slavery is just that and they gonna keep it going one way or another even after President Lincoln calls for an end to it. They're the ones that are in for a rude awakening. The days of slave and master have come and gone whether they're willing to accept it or not."

"We're just going to have to help them used to the idea. But they're not real open to dialogue. Again I stress the need for a more persuasive way of convincing them and for some reason I believe they're more apt to change their thought process staring the nose of a Colt .45 revolver."

We were almost in the quarters now and I had listened and heard and understood both of my lieutenants. Yes. We did need guns and who had most of the guns in Jackson? No other than Jones' General Store who was the biggest gun supplier in the entire county.

In the past year the most we'd acquired was no more than fifteen or twenty firearms. But the gun problem could be dealt with later. Right now we had to deal with the O'Reilly's and that whole situation. There was the old man who was a nasty, drunken Irish ol' cuss and the fruit certainly hadn't fallen far from the tree with his four sons the oldest being Ned. Ned was just as likely hang a niggra than say good morning. But there was not a one of 'em that had an inkling of good in them. They had to be dealt with.

But no matter how I looked at it tomorrow was simply too soon. And then it came to me. The whole gun thing along with the O'Reilly's could be dealt with at the same time. As I spelled it out to Jeremiah and Fiona I watched as their eyes lit up.

The plan was a little more intricate than others we had pulled off but it was possible and so we set it up for the following Friday.

Fridays were usually hectic with the cops and all going in to the general store to be sold and supplies needing to be bought for the upcoming week. And with the construction of the house and tending to Missy's needs there was hardly time to think.

Massa Nicholson usually shut things down around three on a Friday and left me with getting the goods into Jackson for sale. I usually did this after making sure everything was finished at the blacksmithing shop.

Missy would be finishing up making her rounds and would then compile a note of things she needed from the general store. This almost always included laudanum for her back troubles and rheumatism and enough whiskey to get her through the week. She used to ride in with me but since the war had taken a turn for the worse and everyone was in such a depressed state of mind she'd been content to stay at Three Winds.

Today was no different and I started off with nine trusted members of the council sending eight more to the O'Reilly Plantation.

We made the start unusually late giving Jeremiah a chance to carry off his part of the plan a good half an hour before we reached Jackson. Petunia rode in the first buckboard with me sitting in the back while Josiah rode upfront with me playing is usual role as ovaseer in case we were stopped.

Petunia was glad to be away from Three Winds and enjoyed these weekly rides into Jackson and today was no different. Playful as always she poked me in the side several times and pretended Josiah wasn't in attendance with her pointed questions.

"You know Josiah people change when they git a lil authority. Since the colonel been gone off tad a war I don't hardly see my Andrew no more. Miss Missy be

dependin' on Andrew so much nowadays for this and that that he don't eva come see me no more. Now is that any way to treat yo' fiancée Josiah?"

"No ma'am Miss Petunia that ain't hardly no way to treat someone you love and care about," Josiah chimed in.

"You know after a long day of runnin' this way and that and yes ma'am and no ma'am I used to drag my tired ass home and just wanna sit down and cry but I had one thing to keep me goin' and do you know what that was?"

"No ma'am, I sho' don't." Josiah said playfully egging Petunia on.

"I knew my man with his sweaty black body glistening in the sun from a hard day's work was gonna walk in and we was gonna get sex funky and when it was ova I was gonna feel like a brand new woman. Can you unnerstand what ahm sayin' Josiah?"

"I understand completely Miss Petunia. And you're sayin' this to say what?"

"I'm sayin' this man that I am so in love with, that completes me and makes me sing and say that this thang called slavery can't touch the fire that burns bight in my heart and soul has abandoned me. He don't come see me no more. This man that I am to be betrothed to has not only left me but has built himself a new house far away from me. What do you say to that Josiah."

"I would say that that's very unfortunate ma'am and I would certainly make that the next order of business once we have completed this one."

"I do believe you are right Mr. Josiah and I will do just that as soon as this business is completed but I am hopeful that he will come and see me of his own accord tonight and that I will not have to address this issue in my own way which I assure you is not very pleasant."

"For his sake I hope so too Miss Petunia."

I smiled but said nothing.

Just then a plume of smoke arose to the west. They were no more than five minutes out of town now.

Arriving at the general store I saw Jackson was in panic.

"What's going on," Josiah asked as we pulled up at the general store.

"Fire! Looks to be at the O'Reilly place. One of them probably drunk lit the place on fire."

I smiled.

Meanwhile Jeremiah had council members with heads covered waited 'til all five of the O'Reilly's were inside the little log cabin before blasting away and once

pronounced dead proceeded to light both the cabin and barn on fire after distributing most of the livestock to the niggras and taking the horses for council use.

Once both the cabin and barn were ablaze and engulfed in flames they were gone.

Cries of fire at the O'Reilly Place had Jackson residents scurrying and soon the usually bustling town of Jackson was a ghost town. Mr. Jones owner of the general store in his haste to get out to the O'Reilly Place turned to Josiah.

"You know where to unload it. Tell Miss Missy I'll tally her up and give her a total tomorrow, no later than Monday," he said before galloping off in the direction of the O'Reilly Place.

"Such a trusting man," Petunia said grinning as she went through the make-up counter seeing what color lipstick bought out the best in her.

We unloaded quickly and just as quickly loaded up everything we could including close to two hundred rifles and another fifty or so brand new revolvers.

Everything went as smooth as possible. Jeremiah and his men were back in the quarters when we returned. Missy was sound asleep. I still had to go and stash the weapons so I grabbed Jeremiah and the two of us along with Petunia and Fiona went up into the mountains to some old secluded Indian caves up in the mountains to stash the guns. Jeremiah and I would do the unloading and stash the guns but I wanted to get the

girls' opinions on what had just transpired and their thought on how we should move forward.

Petunia was for the most part bright, levelheaded and moderate reminding me a lot of my mother in her council and mirrored my thinking in more cases than not. Well, that was in most cases until the subject of me arose. At these times there was little if no logic or reasoning only blind emotion but I had plans unknowing to her and for now I ignored her impassioned soliloquies and hostility.

Fiona, on the other hand, was militant and brutal in anything concerning her enslavers and the more they whipped her attempting to break her spirit the more bitter and hostile she became. Black and lovely she was dangerous at best but made a fine field general when it came to being disciplined and following orders. I had no problem in commissioning her to carry out retaliatory raids on those that had in some way infringed on the little rights we had.

Jeremiah. Well Jeremiah was simply the embodiment of me contained in a much larger and imposing frame and the mere sight of him for those that didn't know him cast fear in men's eyes both black and white. And in many cases women's too and for that matter women's eyes too.

"Tonight went quite well in my opinion," I said after reaching the caves and unloading the rifles.

"That it did," Jeremiah agreed but tomorrow is really the test. I'm sure Jones's will form a posse and be around to see just what happened. That's the real test. Does everyone have their alibi down pat?"

"I still think we should have gotten rid of Jones amidst all the chaos," Fiona added.

Jeremiah just shook his head.

"That would have really led to speculation and pointed fingers in our direction Right now it just looks like we unloaded the goods and Calvin locked up after we finished and Jones is so arrogant that he would never suspect Calvin of disloyalty or conspiring to rob him. To him Calvin's no more than a simple half-witted niggra. What he doesn't know is that Calvin is a free man and has been all his life and he treats him no better than he treats any other niggra."

61

"Ain't that the truth. I've spoken to him on more than one occasion and teased him about being free. I'd look at him when Massa Jones order him around. 'Didn't you hear the lady boy? She said she needs to ten pound bags of flour. Hurry up you lazy nigga.' I just go over and whisper in his ear, 'so this is what it's like to be a free man? Why I can't see any difference between the way ol' man Jone's treats you and the way m'massa treats me?' And I'd fall out laughing. Calvin would get so angry 'cause he knowed it was true. But what Jones didn't know was how bad Calvin hated him. That's why Calvin joined the council way back when yo' daddy was in charge. And he been a big part on account of those free man's papers that 'llowed him to go and come pretty

much as he pleased. And ever since we freed him from the patrollers that caught him and said he was a runaway t'aint a thing he won't do when it comes to the council."

"Damn you ornery Petunia. You always teasin' and makin' fun of somebody," Fiona said laughing.

"I don't tease or make fun of you though even though I knows you done been sleepin' with m'fiancee," she laughed.

"And will every chance I get," she laughed.

"And you know one day I'm gonna have to kill you for that," Petunia laughed.

"It's well worth it," Fiona laughed.

"I know that's right but not tonight. If Missy don't have plans for his black ass he's all mine. And for some unknown reason I don't believe Missy too worried about Andrew tonight after that double dose of sleep medicine I gave her," Petunia said still laughing.

"You be careful with her Andrew. She's crazy as a Betsy bug."

I smiled.

"So, we all have our alibis ready?"

Everyone nodded.

"Then everyone make sure that we go about our normal jobs and steer clear of each other. Josiah went to see his people up in the mountains for a couple of days and the next council meeting will be held on Thursday. I'll send a runner over to the O'Reilly place to see how ol' Ben and his people are faring tomorrow night if all is quiet."

"And I'm going to see you when we get back?" Petunia asked.

"I'm thinking I could be your alibi."

"Good possibility but for now let's get these horses and buckboards put away without causing too much of a disturbance.

Once we had everything put away I went up to Magnolia House and laid down next to Missy as if I'd been there all along. I nudged her twice.

"Oh, Andrew I 'm so sorry I must have fallen asleep on you. It's the medicine you know. I must have taken too strong a dose. You can take me if you want me."

Moments later, she was snoring softly and I made my way out the back to rejoin Petunia who was waiting patiently. I noticed the sudden change in her demeanor and knew better than to ask why. After a few minutes walking hand-in-hand towards the quarters she spoke.

"Why is it that they think they can do whatever they please to us?"

"Who are you talking about dear?" I asked knowing full well who she was referring to.

"You know damn well who I'm referring to Andrew. Missy, that's who, that white bitch has spent the last ten years making life miserable for every niggra on Three Winds. She's no different than any of the rest of them white folks. She's greed and selfish. She don't look at us any differently than she looks at a good plow horse. The only thing she sees is how we can serve her and how much work she can get out of us. To her we're not humans. We have no hearts, no souls, no feelings. And if it's not enough to work you from can't see in the morning 'til can't see at night now she wants you to act as her bed warmer at night. It doesn't matter that I'm in love with you. The only thing that matters is that you love her to sleep every night. How can she be so unfeeling, so uncaring? She must know that you don't have any feelings for her with her almighty, aristocratic white ass. And with all her money and power how must she feel to have to sleep with someone she believes to be beneath her?"

I just shook my head. Petunia was simply stating what I'd been thinking about over the last month or so. And like Petunia I had no answers and told her so.

"I hear you. Not that I'm interested in changing her ideas or thoughts but what bothers me most is the possibility that she really and truly believes that whites folks are superior. You can't honestly think that she really believes that she's superior when she is

so dependent on us for not just her lifestyle but her life. Without us she couldn't survive. We could but she couldn't. In a way I think she knows that. That's why she agreed to give us the land just to keep us on. I'm certain it didn't have anything to do with conscience or the fact that she could for once in her life do something out of kindness."

"Hell no. The woman has no conscience but like you said the fact that she agreed is her own testimony that she can't exist without us. It may even go further than that and just be a testament to your lovin'. For the first time in her life she's found a man that truly makes her feel like a woman. A woman will give the moon and the sky to feel that way. Me, I want to feel that way every day. Which brings up another matter?"

"Let's not start with that Petunia. Let's just enjoy the time we have together. Who knows what tomorrow may bring."

"I starting to believe you're just afraid of commitment Andrew Jackson."

"Or maybe I'm just afraid of you."

"Seriously though Andrew, what are you going to do about Missy?"

64

"Well, right now she's probably the closest thing to an ally that we have. You and I both know that. So, we'll ride it as far as we can."

"How is she?"

"Right through here I'd say she's confused. She has a husband that she is pretty adamant about. She's aware that he doesn't want her and only uses her because she's easy on the eyes. He can present her in certain circles but neither wants her as a friend, partner or lover and like any woman she wants to feel loved and needed. He doesn't get it done. He has no use for her and she none for him. And right now she is happier without him and has made it plain that he won't be returning from the war."

"Did she say that?"

"Made it quite plain and in no uncertain terms she did."

"What's she going to do?"

"That she's unwilling to say. But she has assured me that he won't be returning. I think she's planning to have him killed. That's the impression I get which will be fine."

"Yes. Then we won't have to."

"Exactly."

"But you still haven't told me. How is she?"

"I'm not following you."

"How is she in bed?"

"Like a love sick puppy. Clumsy and starving. Hungry and eager. The woman hasn't been with anyone for seven or eight years so you can imagine."

"I don't even want to think about something like that. It's been close to a month and I'm about to die. I couldn't even imagine a year let alone seven or eight years. Three weeks and I'm on fire."

"Come on sweetheart. Let me quench that fire for you."

"You realize that he white woman will have you killed should anyone find out that you're sleeping with her. She'd die just to keep her reputation intact."

"I know Petunia."

"And then I'd have to kill her."

I loved that woman and she took comfort in knowing it as I did. We had been a couple ever since I could remember with her stepping out only when she would get frustrated when I refused to marry her. But in the last few months we'd been more involved than ever. Still, with my blacksmithing responsibilities, checking on mama, the council and now Missy's constant demands I hardly had time. We spent the night together that night and or the first time in a long time I could relax.

The time to relax quickly ended as Monday came roaring in. First there was the sheriff and his men.

"Miss Missy ma'am I'm not sure if you're aware or not but the general store was robbed last night."

"Oh, my God. Was it the Yanks? Damn Yankees!"

"No ma'am. Confederate Army's still holding them at bay. We think someone right here in the area may have done it. O'Reilly Place was burned to the ground at approximately the same time. Killed the ol' man and his sons. We think the fire at the

O'Reilly's was a diversionary tactic. As you know the O'Reilly's were a bit hard on their slaves which leads us to believe that this may have been in retaliation and while the town rushed to the aid of the O'Reilly's over two hundred guns were stolen from the Jones' General Store."

"I'm sorry to hear that sheriff but why is this any of my concern?"

"Well, a few of your hands made a delivery to the general store according to Mr. Jones and he left while they were still unloading your goods Miss Missy."

"And your point is?"

"Well, I'm not saying that they had anything to do with it but they may have seen something out of the ordinary."

"No, sheriff, they went as instructed and dropped off our crops to market the same way they do each and every Friday and returned promptly."

"Well, do you mind if I speak to them just to make sure?"

"I do mind. I will not lose valuable harvesting by having them come out of the fields to answer questions that you already have the answers to. You know as well as I do that there are no slaves in the county capable of pulling off what you have just described to me."

"Miss Missy ma'am I don't know if you know or not but there have been quite a few rather sophisticated slave uprisings in the last few years. Now I'm in agreement with you that a niggra ain't hardly capable of putting nothin' like this together but with abolitionists running around along with a lot of Northern sympathizer's right here in our midst anything's possible. You put two hundred guns in the hands of niggra slaves and that could give Sherman just the advantage he needs."

"I assure you sheriff m'niggras ain't had nothin' to do with it. I just parceled out close to two thousand acres to them to keep 'em on the place when the war ends. So, I think you're barking up the wrong tree."

The sheriff hearing this sat there in shock.

"Afternoon ma'am," he said tipping his hat before turning the big bay hose and riding off at a gallop.

I too stood staring in disbelief. Turning to look at me I hardly recognized her.

"Is there something you want to tell me Andrew?"

"Uh, yes ma'am," I said pausing to take a deep breath before continuing. "Massa Jones said he would send you the final tally. He was in too much of a rush—him rushing to get to the fire and all—to tally up last night."

"Anything else?"

"No ma'am. I reckon that's it. It's pretty much as you told the sheriff. Ain't no different than any other Friday delivery." I whispered hoping not to give myself away but the way missy looked at me let me know that she had come to know me better than I thought and I knew it wouldn't be the last I'd heard of the matter.

Later that day Massa Jones came riding in not nearly so nice as the sheriff had been.

He and Missy had always been friendly on account of him and the colonel was close friends but you would never have known that by the way he rode in.

"Believe your niggas robbed my store missy."

"And how are you today Mr. Jones?" Missy replied ignoring Massa Jones rudeness.

"Them niggas you sent in last night robbed my store. Stole over two hundred of my finest rifles. And I want them back. Them niggas is gonna hang for this. I want to see them all now. I'm taking them back into Jackson with me so they can all be tried and hung. Teach 'em to steal from me."

"Mr. Jones I don't appreciate your tone and if the colonel were here he'd have you hog tied and thrown off Three Winds just for the discourteous way in which you rode in here and spoke to his wife. Furthermore, those are the same niggras that have been coming to market for the last ten years. They are some of my most trusted niggras and I don't appreciate you accusing my niggras of anything. Now where is my money and a tally for the crops delivered to you last night?"

"They stole that too along with the rifles."

"And I am to believe that these same niggras that supposedly robbed your store stole the crops that they delivered Mr. Jones? Really? I want a receipt and payment for the crops by this Friday. I am quite sorry for your loss but where I am from a gentlemen is always a gentlemen regardless of the stress and turmoil that life brings him. Once that is done please tally up all past debt and monies which you owe Three Winds which I am sure amounts to quite a bit more than a few measly rifles. I want that paid in full as well. You have one week Mr. Jones. And have it duly noted that we will be taking our business to Vicksburg from now on. I'm not sure of the market there but I am sure that they are much more courteous. Now if there's nothing else I want you off my land."

By this time a small crowd had gathered and I don't know if missy knew it or not she had at that moment become a friend of the niggra. When Massa Jones I breathed a deep sigh of relief and went on with my shoeing of a horse brought in by one of the O'Reilly's a day or so ago.

Yet, despite her dismissal of both the sheriff and Massa Jones I could get no clear indication of what missy was feeling or thinking and so I summoned Petunia from the kitchen.

"How's she doing?"

"Strong as I ever seen her. It's time for her midday toddy but when I asked her if she was ready for it she just brushed me aside. Said 'not today Petunia'. Hard to figger. You might wanna to talk to her. She seems out-of-sorts. Almost normal like. That's what's so scary. Nobody changes overnight like that."

I heard Petunia but said nothing but felt the same way and feeling eyes on us I looked up to find Missy staring at us through an upstairs window. I said a few more words to Petunia before heading back to the blacksmith shop. No sooner than I got there I heard feet approaching.

69

"I need to speak to you privately."

"Now?"

"Right now."

"Finish that horse and then stat on the gray sorrel," I said to my young apprentice as I followed missy up on to the front porch.

"I have several pressing things on my mind Andrew as you can probably guess but I want to begin with your whereabouts last night."

"You know where I was last night Missy," I said forgetting myself.

"Well, it's nice to see you've finally gotten over the formalities.

"Now please tell me where you were last night."

"I did the same thing I do every Friday night. I took the cops in to Massa Jones…"

"I know that Andrew!" she said her voice rising slightly. "I'm talking afterwards."

"Why I came back here. Don't you remember me talking to you?"

"Yes, I remember and then where did you go?"

"Why I went back down to the quarters after you dismissed me saying you had taken a bit too much of your medicine."

There was a long pause. When Missy spoke again there was a gentler tone.

"And where did you go when you went back down to the quarters?"

"Ma'am?"

"You heard me Andrew."

"Why I went to Petunia's."

"And you spent the night with her?"

"Yes, ma'am."

"You were engaged to be married to her?"

"Yes ma'am."

"And you two have feelings for each other?"

"I suppose."

"That's over Andrew. Do you understand me? There is no wrath like a woman's and from this day on you belong to me and I refuse to share another man. Now if she can benefit you more than I can then I suggest you choose Petunia. But you and I know she cannot and your goal of saving your people will need a great deal more than what Petunia can offer so you will let her go. Is that understood?"

"I hear you."

"I know you hear me Andrew but what's more important is that you understand. I will have the black whipped off her if you do not comply. I will have her face cut and disfigured 'til you will not recognize her and she will be ashamed t show herself in public and she far too pretty a girl for you to subject her to that. So, say your goodbyes but not a word will be passed between you after today. Understood?"

"But may I ask why ma'am?"

"Because I knew when the sheriff was talking to me that you were responsible for the O'Reilly fire and their deaths and the general store robbery. I knew. And I also knew that there was no way I was letting him get his hands on the man that I loved. I knew right then and there that I loved you and I would defend you with my life if necessary. And just like I will not let any white man touch you I don't want anyone else touching what I claim to be mine; woman or man no matter what color they are and that goes for Petunia and Fiona. You want things for your people. Then you come to me. There is no longer any need to rob and pillage and burn. But these are the stipulations. You will be devoted to my pleasure and my pleasure only. Do we have a deal?"

"Shall we shake on it?"

"We'll shake later behind closed doors," she said smiling.

"But Missy you know Petunia looks after m'mama when I'm not around."

"Find someone else and not nearly so attractive. I'll see you at eight and we can talk about your plans for those rifles," she said as she walked away.

At seven I met Petunia down in the quarters along with Jeremiah and Petunia and spelled out everything.

"So, Missy's no fool?" Jeremiah said.

"I could have told you that long ago when the colonel was still around. She seem like she ain't in touch but she's been on top of things for some time now. She got her own set of books aside from Three Winds and takes almost a quarter of everything Thee Winds brings in and has it invested in something in Boston though I can't rightly figger what it is but I know she has quite a lot of money stashed away up there.

Truth is if she ever got upset she could have the whole lot of us killed and not have a second thought."

"The fact that she would have Petunia's face disfigured is okay with me. And the idea that she wants this heifer out of the picture also appeals to my sensibilities but the fact that she wants both of us out of the picture strikes me as wrong especially since Petunia has never actually threatened my well-being. But seriously speaking Andrew I understand what she's offering and it's a dangerous game. I think you need to work hard and fast and get all the basic essentials for our people and then be done with her before she gets or has us all killed. For one thing she knows too much."

72

"I agree. We simply need the necessities and we have most of that now. And soon as things calm down we need to blow the whistle on her illegal activities."

"Let's just play it by ear," Jeremiah said. "We need to take our time. I suggest we place armed guards at the entrance to Three Winds. Josiah and his sons and keep a

runner close by around the clock to warn Andrew of any intruders so he doesn't get caught with his pants down and keep her happy as long as we can."

"And what about me?" Petunia asked.

"And what about you?" Jeremiah replied. "Since when did your happiness overshadow the three hundred?"

"You know what the council does to people that think like that and put themselves before the good of the many."

"The proposed sentence is…"

"Death," Petunia replied. "Even in freedom we must still bow down to them."

"Our faith tells us that the meek will inherit the earth," I replied.

"Doesn't necessarily say in my lifetime," Petunia retorted.

"Have faith sweetheart. Our time is approaching," Jeremiah said grabbing Petunia and holding her close.

A month or so later the house I had fashioned for myself was completed and though it was a fine house with its two white marble pillars. And when it was first built I thought it a bit too grand and high falutin' for a common field hand like myself but as the

days passed it paled in comparison to the houses my fellow slaves were constructing all over Three Winds. Men, my fellow slaves would work from sun up to sun down toiling in the fields and at night committees would get together—sometimes as many as thirty or forty men-too help their neighbors with this new undertaking and soon brand new homes peppered the once barren landscape. My home as I said paled in contrast.

Mama's house was one of the first to go up thanks to the council and in memory of the work my pappy had done on behalf of these men. Mama was tickled. And when the men sought to build a garden my mama wouldn't have it proclaiming how she'd spent too much time as a field hand. He last think she wanted to see was another field so close to home. But the flowers that surrounded the house in every color and shade made up for the peas and corn.

Missy seemed happy too. Things were and continued to be even more prosperous than ever before at Three Winds and the men began working in shifts and work they did.

Seeing the growing prosperity it was becoming easier by the day to convince Missy of new ideas and with little or no prompting we soon had a rather thriving horse and cattle ranch where the lower forty had once been.

All seemed to be going quite well and Missy seemed to be as happy as any southern white woman could be in spite of the South's precarious position. I, on the

other hand was still puzzled by Missy. Her sudden sobriety did nothing to placate my uneasiness. Less predictable than she'd been it wasn't unusual for her to show up at random now that she was established as a friend of the niggra. And once or twice a hush fell over a council meeting when she'd show up unexpectedly. She was even more demanding of me now that she was sober and insisted on me being with her at all times now and I actually created work for myself just to keep her away. And she could not do enough in her attempts to make me happy which was all well and good but it came at a price I found harder and harder to pay.

More and more I came to regret the agreement I'd bought into but then what had been my options. Many a night I found myself to tired to honor my agreement and would walk into this monstrosity of a house she'd

74

insisted on having me build climb the stairs only to find her naked and grinning in my bed. After too many a night of trying to shoo her away and warning her of the danger if someone were to find us in bed together I gave up.

One day when Jeremiah and I had the occasion to sneak away I told him of my misfortune.

"That is the cost of selling your soul to the devil," he laughed. "Do you realize how long it's been since you promised Petunia that once our folks were settled in and doing well that you would marry her?"

I could not remember.

"And do you remember what she decreed when she took you with her to see the judge and had deeds for two hundred slaves made legal?"

"That I do remember. She made me the sole heir to Three Winds at the time of her death."

"That she did after the mysterious death of the colonel which you and I both know was no accident."

I nodded.

"You used to steal away with Petunia despite her threats. And because you had a certain affinity—which I still believe you have—you would steal away with Fiona. Now she has you so closely watched you cannot steal away from yourself. Do you know what that tells me Andrew?"

"I'm listening."

"That it is time that you make your promises—as hard as it may seem—come to fruition. You owe it to Petunia, you owe it to Fiona but most of all you owe it to yourself. You freed those folks over at the O'Reilly Plantation long before Lincoln was killed and proclaimed emancipation. You freed us here and gave us prosperity like no niggra has in the North and in the South. You have armed us and trained us for those who seek reprisal. You have educated us and built a fine school and church. You have made us not only free but self-sufficient at the risk of remaining in bondage yourself. Now Andrew it is time for you to throw the shackles off and enjoy the freedom which you have shown us."

"And how do you propose I do that Jeremiah?"

"Listen we have travelled a long way together and I am here because of the many things you have taught me. Do not pretend that you have forgotten? It is time for you to throw the shackles off."

"I will have Fiona prepare the tea once you give me the word. She has done many a good deed for us. Her death will not be painful. I only await your word."

"Have it done," I said careful not to give it any more thought. It was inevitable. It needed to be done.

I sat for what seemed like hours at the little creek I loved so much when I was just a boy. I listened to the water as it rushed making clapping sounds on the rocks. Here I came to seek solace and think and meditate but there was no solace now.

Slowly, I rose and made my way back to Magnolia knowing that Jeremiah was right. Her time had come. Killing her would release me from the last throes of bondage and free Fiona and Petunia too but how could I in lieu of all that she had done not only on

my behalf but on behalf of Three Winds and the three hundred slaves that had been under the servitude of her husband the colonel.

She had killed him and freed them against insurmountable odds. She'd protected me and stood tall on my behalf when they wanted to hang me. She'd known I masterminded the robbery and had never questioned me about the guns or their whereabouts knowing that I would not do anything foolish with them that would jeopardize either of us. And she had done everything to make me happy, to make me love her. Now here I was faced with the idea of killing her.

Climbing the stairs I only prayed she wasn't there tonight.

"I've waited so long for you m'darling," she said her gown giving way to her small protruding breast which fell out and hang dangling. "I guess she's glad to see you too," she said smiling. "What's wrong darling? Is it something I said? "she said smiling and crawling towards me on the bed.

"No, Melissa. I just have a lot on my mind."

"Well, come here darling let mama help ease your mind," she said grabbing at my belt.

"No missy. Not tonight."

"Oh my. That bad is it? Well let me share something that may ease all your worries away."

"Please do," I said knowing that no matter what she said would do little to forego the inevitable. "What is it?"

"I'm going to have your child Andrew."

Part Two

This latest bit of news was shocking to say the least. I remember back when I was just a small lad after my mama tore into my father for some miniscule oversight on his part. At the time I had a hard time understanding why he tolerated it.

This was soon after he introduced me to the council where literally hundreds of men revered my father and looked at him as a leader, a chief, a general entrusted to lead them through the gates of hell if he saw fit. And yet my mother, a diminutive woman who stood no more than four feet eleven had this monstrous hold over him.

When she'd finished berating him soundly he walked out of tiny cabin and lit his corn cob pipe and looked to the heavens as if pleading to the good Lord to give him the strength to endure his plight.

I could never understand. That is up until today when I stared at this diminutive white woman I felt so indebted to that I was willing to give up my very freedom for and live in purgatory with for the rest of my days.

This of course was against my very constitution and my advisors had all recommended the same course of action when it came to her. She had despite her recent epiphany been a part of all the misery and suffering niggras at Three Winds over the past decade. And though most had received a more than gracious reprieve I alone was still suffering at the hands of this woman and yet I was the one who questioned whether she

should meet her maker sooner than later. Now with this latest bit of news I was once again completely baffled and dumbfounded.

I thought of my father with his corncob pipe in one hand staring up at the heavens for answers, for his own sort of reprieve and asked.

"Father, you who command the respect of so many men, strong men, soldiers and the like why then do you permit this tiny woman to command you?"

My father who never answered anything quickly stood there staring before turned to me and smiled.

"One day you will understand my son. Man may control all things on this earth but if it is one thing that has control over man aside from God it is a woman. Woman controls man. You will learn once you are older that she is our cross to bear."

I now understood my father's words.

"My goodness Andrew. That certainly wasn't the kind of response I was anticipating.
        "I'm sorry Missy. You were saying?"

"I was saying we are going to have a baby Andrew. The whole time I was married to the colonel the doctor's ruled it out. They said it wasn't possible but don't you see it was.

Don't you see Andrew? It wasn't me at all. If you ask me I have a different theory but I could never have shared it with John. I've always believed that baby's were conceived out of love and there was no love between John and I and that's why conception wasn't possible. And darling that's why we have a child on the way. Come here sweetheart. Come hold me."

Nestled in my arms she was soon fast asleep.

My head was spinning as I made my way out of the house and bumped into Fiona.

"Hello Andrew."

"Fiona," I said nodding. My head was ablaze with all the recent news.

"Thought we were spending some time together last night?"

"I'm sorry Fiona. I had my hands full last night."

"She is a handful isn't she?"

"That she is," I said searching for my pipe.

"Did she tell you the news?"

"What news?"

"That she's pregnant."

"Yes," I said before thinking and shocked that Fiona knew. "Come around to the other side of the house before she sees us talking. So, she told you she was pregnant."

81

"Of course not. Petunia and I see her every morning when she comes down for breakfast and soon as she smells the food that morning sickness kicks in. She tried to tell us she was coming down with something. But we both know the symptoms. And you know how devilish Petunia is. She's just begging to ask her if it's the colonel's baby and if not whose is it?"

I had to smile.

"You keep a muzzle on that ol' crazy gal." I said.

"So, she told you huh?"

"Yeah, just now."

"I guess that's why you look so out-of-it?"

"Yeah, really threw me a curve."

"And you still want me to go ahead with the plan?"

"I don't rightly know Fiona. Let me sleep on it but you can do me a favor and give her a dose with her dinner. I do believe I have a prior engagement," I sad winking at her before walking away.

"Andrew."

"Yeah, Fiona?"

"You know I don't have any problem with extending her sleep permanently if it means seeing more of you. I miss the old days."

I smiled and continued walking. The night air felt good as I thought about the old days working alongside my father and then sneaking away for a couple of hours to spend time with my girls or go fishing with Jeremiah. Seemed like those days were long gone and in their stead a world full of dilemma. But if there was anyone who would understand and empathize with me it was Jeremiah.

I found him down at the old watering hole where we'd hide our jugs of moonshine. He was quite inebriated when I walked up behind him. With a big grin he waved me over and handed me the jug.

"Looks like you need it. What's going on old man? You look like you have the weight of the world on your head."

"Don't know what it looks like but it sure feels like I do. I guess you heard?"

"Yeah, I heard this morning right after you left. Wouldn't want to be in your spot my friend. So, what are you going to do? The dynamics have certainly changed."

"Don't know. Thought maybe you and I can toss it around and come up with something."

"Sorry Andrew. Not this time. This one's all on you. I don't want to give you any advice that may affect the rest of your life."

"Understood. But you know that living under the current situation is bound to be lethal. There is already speculation among our folks and if there is it's only a matter of time before the word gets out. She's already hated among many of the slaveholders for parceling out land to niggras. They're already calling her a nigga lover. But if they were to get a whiff of the notion that she was sleepin' with a niggra they'd burn Three Winds to the ground and hang every niggra on it. That's the bottom line."

"We have been aware of that since day one Andrew. But now you have coupled that with the fact that you have a conscience my friend and you know despite all the rhetoric about white folks being the devil you've found that this is a good woman and you my friend have made her recognize the goodness within herself. And she is grateful to you for that. Now she is happy and her being happy has had a profound effect on all of us. We have benefited from her generosity and her love for you. And her love for you has evolved into a child.

Now the question you have to ask yourself as a man but more importantly as a leader of men is if the weight of one worth the weight of many. It is a simple question and child or no child you know the answer. It doesn't change anything. The longer you prolong the inevitable the more danger you put not only yourself in but all of us."

I knew Jeremiah was right. I knew the answer before I even asked him but I had to hear it. And now I had to act. I guess I wasn't so different from everyone else at Three Winds. I too had come to love this white woman.

"May God forgive me. Not only will I be killing a woman but my unborn child as well," I said now weeping outright.

"Jesus wept too my friend."

I sat there long after Jeremiah made his leave. I prayed that Jesus would understand, guide and forgive me and when I had no more tears left and the sky was littered with stars I found my way to Fiona's cabin where I cried some more.

"I share your pain Andrew but if I can say this to you in attempts to ease your pain and sorrow but the day you don't grieve over taking a life is the day you stop being the man that I have come to love and respect. And if it makes you feel any better you have no choice. If you let her live until she has the baby you will only feel worse for having killed the child's mother. No, Andrew you are doing the right thing. She is sleeping soundly. In the morning I will send her to her final resting place."

"No, Fiona this burden rests on my shoulders. This weight is for me to carry alone. I will be the one to do this."

"As you wish."

"And what is it that you wish for Fiona?"

"Only that I can provide you with some happiness tonight."

"You've already done that."

"Then let me see what I can do to add to that."

I dreaded the morning but there was no avoiding it. The skies were overcast and dreary as was my mood. Entering Magnolia House Fiona and Petunia both greeted me like I was the Grim Reaper himself. The fact that Missy's murder was agreed on by the council as the necessary thing to do made it no easier on any of us.

I even considered telling Missy that her life depended on her giving me back my own but when I approached the subject she flew into such a rage saying she would rather die than to lose me she signed her own death warrant.

She had long since forgotten protocol and when I walked into the kitchen she rushed over, kissed me flush on the lips and went on about how she missed my warmth by her side last night.

Fiona gazed at me and I read her stare. It was just such behavior that would lead to me my hanging.

"Coffee Missy?"

"Yes, dear two sugars and a dash of milk thank you."

With my back to her and Fiona distracting her I added an extra teaspoon of sugar to shadow the taste of the laudanum which I added rather liberally before handing the cup to her.

"Aren't you going to sit and share a cup with me?"

"Can't today. Mr. Will's due here at ten and I still have two of his horses needing shod."

"Lunch then?"

"Lunch it is," I said tears filling my eyes knowing that I was seeing Missy for the last time.

An hour later Petunia found me tending the horses.

"She's gone Andrew," Petunia said her tears stained from crying. "She was so mean to me. I don't know why I'm going on like this."

There was no need to explain. I think we shared the same sentiment.

"Where is she?"

"Fiona and I carried her upstairs and put her to bed just like you said. We took the left the open bottle of laudanum next to her and we sent Josiah in to get the doctor. He should be here within the next half hour or so."

"Good. Good."

"I don't think I need to be anywhere around so I'm going to grab mama and go pick strawberries."

"I'll call you if we need you, sweetheart and don't you worry. Fiona and I can handle Doc Rivers."

Later that evening I walked back down to watering hole and leaned back against the old willow. I was exhausted but had too much on my mind to sleep. Not long after Fiona and Petunia joined me.

"The doctor and the sheriff stopped by and pronounced Missy dead seemingly from a self-administered overdose of laudanum. And the sheriff said after looking over her will that you need to go in and see the judge to have everything formalized in the morning," Fiona recounted.

"You didn't tell me that she left you Three Winds. The woman must have really loved you Andrew," Petunia said. "It's kind of hard to compete with that."

I didn't want either of them to feel any worse than they were already feeling so I changed the subject.

"Now that we have one of the largest plantations in Mississippi at our disposal and more money than any of us ever dreamed of what do you propose we do with it?"

"Let's not our chicken's before their hatched," came Jeremiah's voice from the trees. "Folks are feeling a certain kind of way about Missy's death. White folks are saying that Missy wasn't herself after the colonel's death. If she had been she would never have signed forty thousand acres over to a nigga. They're gonna fight it Andrew."

"I expected that. That's what we prepared for isn't it. How many trained soldiers do we have here at Three Winds?"

"A little over two hundred."

"And the rest of the plantations?"

"Maybe another couple of hundred at best but I can't say how ready they are?"

"All I know is they're armed. They're still under the same regime as before so they really don't have the freedom to train the way we do here."

"Understood."

"The Freedmen's Bureau took over the O'Reilly Place after the war and did pretty much the same thing you did here and parceled the land off and Ol' Ben's been following the same script you've had for here so they're in good shape and the place is looking a whole better than when them Irish drunks owned it."

"Couldn't help but improve."

"But let's get back to your situation. Townspeople want to have the funeral in two days and the undertakers up at the house already preparing the body. But tomorrow's when you go into Jackson to put your mark on the will and deed and assume ownership of Three Winds. There's gonna be a lotta angry white folks lining the streets to see who this niggra is that was so highly thought of by this white woman that she gave him forty thousand acres of the best land in these here parts. Half of it will be jealousy and the rest will be sheer bigotry and hatred. I want you in and out of there with the quickness. I'm sending Josiah and his sons in there with you as bodyguards and to give the impression that they are still

87

running things. But expect the worst. And just get your Black ass back to us safely."

"Understood."

"I've doubled the guard around the place for the next few weeks. I have a feeling the nightriders are gonna want to put some fear into us in trying to take back this land."

"Thank you Jeremiah," I said deeply moved by this.

"Figgered you had your hands full with the whole missy thing."

"And your troubles are just beginning," Petunia chimed in. "Our folks, though they respect you really believe that you were no more than a bug in Missy's ear on their behalf. They respect you but half of them don't know and the other half don't believe that a niggra has the capacity to manage anything without the white folks. It's sad but we've been brainwashed into thinking that we're not capable of doing anything but waiting on others. You're going to have to step in as soon as you get back and Missy's buried and make a wide spread decree to let 'em know you're in charge."

"Already considered that long before Missy passed. I have some things I'd like to implement. Nothing major but I am going to make changes. The first thing I want to do is tear Magnolia House down and use the remnants to build a school and make education mandatory for Three Winds and O'Reilly. Then we're going to rework the deeds for all the niggras who hold land on Three Winds. In order to continue to continue school will be mandatory up until the age of sixteen. Upon completion I want every male and female to do a two year apprenticeship in a number of areas including the military so we can become autonomous and self-sufficient. The council will also be opened up to those who would willingly seek membership and will act as the governing council."

Petunia smiled.

"I see you've been doing your homework," Petunia countered. "And since you've given this so much thought I have one more question."

88

"Ask me," I said feeling supremely confident.

"Now that Missy's gone and there is nothing else in the way when are you going to put Fiona out to pasture with the rest of the heifers and set a date lover?"

If anyone could throw me for a loop it was Petunia who stood there grinning as I stood there dumbfounded.

"Let's just get through this latest upheaval," I said trying my best to avoid this latest barrage of questions. In truth, I hadn't given it any thought.

I enjoyed Petunia for her quick wit and mischievousness. She was extremely bright with a voracious appetite for books and knowledge in general and was easy on the eye. Fiona, by contrast had an easy going manner and though she may not have been Petunia's intellectual peer she ran circles around her when it came to common sense. Jet black her Egyptian like features and utter beauty made many a white man and black gasp upon first seeing her.

I favored both depending on the day and enjoyed the best of both and it was always Petunia who sought more. Fiona may have felt the same way but had yet to voice it in all the years I'd known her.

"I want you to ride in with Andrew tomorrow," Jeremiah said staring directly at Fiona.

"And how did you come about that decision?" Petunia asked petulantly.

"That's the reason precisely," Jeremiah said rather-of-factly. "You're far too high strung. Your temper will be all of our undoing Petunia. What we need tomorrow is calm reserve; someone to act coolly under pressure. I want you to pack that little pearl handled .22 but use it under no circumstances unless they try to harm you or my friend. Is that understood?"

"Perfectly," Fiona said ignoring Petunia.

"And I suggest you come to some sort of agreement on how you plan to coexist. This man you say you care about so much has the weight of the world on his shoulders right through here."

We walked back stronger for the meeting—well that is—except for Petunia who hummed Closer My God to Thee as she stared at Fiona the entire time. I took it as an idle threat since the two had been the best of friends since they were little. And although both had killed several times at the council's request Petunia had no stomach for it whereas Fiona seemed to relish her assignments and was quite proficient at it. No, Fiona was the wrong person to threaten.

Walking through the homes now plastered along the landscape we came across several persons who had just gotten the news of Missy's passing actually crying and I wondered how they could have forgotten so quickly the fear and cruelty she had imposed on niggras not more than a couple of years ago.

The four of us made it up to my home after Jeremiah made sure that the guards were stationed at their posts. Fiona and Petunia then prepared a most delicious dinner of duck, ham, green beans, stuffing and a peach cobbler that was absolutely delicious before we convened to the front porch to smoke and talk of our good fortune.

Fiona who worked as a midwife left to make her rounds and Jeremiah not wanting to feel like a third wheel walked her.

"Guess that just leaves you and me. You realize this is the first time Fiona and I have been here."

"I didn't realize."

"The wicked witch of the west forbade us to come near you let alone step foot in this house."

I smiled thinking how obsessed and possessive Missy had become.

"She was a mess wasn't she?"

"And one that won't be sorely missed. If these ignorant niggras around here crying only knew. But that's past history. Let's start our own history by you giving me a tour of the house and let's christen each room on the way," she said pulling me into the house and then the living where she kissed and began undressing me. By the time we finally hit the bedroom we had all we could do to roll back the sheets and crawl in.

It was then, at that moment that I knew that I had to make a decision soon.

Monday morning came in with the thunder of horses. Petunia was still asleep. I grabbed my rifle and peered through the window. It was the Josiah boys with their daddy at the lead and Fiona with the carriage.

I preferred the buckboard and made it be known/\. Minutes later Josiah's sons were back and we were on our way. The air hung heavy and there was little conversation.

"How you feeling Andrew," Fiona asked.

"No worse for the wear. How are you this morning?"

"Okay. Anxious to get this over with," she said whipping the horses into a lather.

We rode most of the way in a comfortable silence before Fiona spoke again.

"Andrew you know I am always concerned with your welfare and I know the pressure you've had on you as leader of the council since your father passed and so I try to do no more than be there for you. And I think I've done that. But now that this day has come and Missy is no longer a part of our lives where do we stand. I mean what is my role to be as you see it?"

"I'm still working that out Fiona. I'm thinking about Petunia in charge of the school and Jeremiah in charge of the council. I haven't quite decided what role will best suit us. You have so many talents that I don't want to pigeonhole you. I was thinking of starting a hospital and putting you in charge but then I would need you to help me run things and do the books so I don't know."

Fiona smiled and whipped the horses harder. And for some reason I knew the horses were being whipped out of her frustration for me.

"Sometimes I want to say you're the brightest man I know. And then there are times like these."

No sooner had Fiona mouthed those words there came a loud pop with two or more in rapid succession causing the horses to rear up throwing both Fiona and myself from the buckboard. Josiah's youngest son, Justice hit the ground with a thud and screamed out in pain. I grabbed Fiona and dragged her towards the trees and cover before going back and doing the same for .

"Everyone okay?" shouted Josiah. "Which way are the shots coming from?" but there were no more shots. "Think someone was just trying to scare off," he said helping his son to his feet. Whatcha want to do Andrew?"

"What did we come to do?"

"Okay then. If everybody's okay mount up."

I was sure Justice's arm was broken but he was not going to miss out and rejoined the party doing his best to ask his injury.

"You okay Fiona?"

"No worse for the wear. No one said progress came without a little adversity," she said smiling.

We arrived in Jackson twenty minutes later and I proceeded into the judge's office at a little after eight. A plump middle aged southern gentleman he greeted me cordially.

"Mr. Andrew it is good to see you although I wouldn't say garner to say that isn't the majority opinion in Jackson this morning," he laughed. "It is a sad occasion though with Missy's passing and all."

"It is indeed. She will be sadly missed."

"Still she had the foresight to will you her estate in attempts of rectifying past ills and atrocities on behalf of herself and her late husband."

"If you say so judge…"

"You don't agree?"

"I'm not the person you should be addressing that to judge. Perhaps you should tell that to the good folks of Jackson that tried to shoot us on the way in to see you today."

The judge stopped and just stared at me.

"Oh, my God! Was anyone hurt?"

"No, your honor."

"You know I had a feeling that this whole issue of a niggra being one of the largest landowners in the county wouldn't go over well with the local residents but I never would have expected anything like this. Don't mean to be meddlesome but I would keep everything pretty low key until these people get used to the idea of a niggra landholder."

"Thanks judge. The advice is appreciated but could you hurry with those papers. I wanna get out of Jackson as soon as possible."

The judge handed me a thick stack of papers and I knew as liberal and good as the judge was he wasn't shaking a niggras hand.

"We good?" Fiona asked as I exited the judge's chambers.

"I suppose but I'll feel a whole lot better when we get to Three Winds," I said. Fiona whipped the horses into a lather and Josiah and his boys fell in alongside of us. I think everyone tensed up when we passed the spot where the shots had been fired earlier. There were no shots this time and I sent Justice ahead to round up everyone.

Arriving there I found a large crowd gathered and smiles and congratulations from everyone.

"Folks this is the first niggra plantation in all of Mississippi. But we don't want to be known as just the first niggra plantation. We want to be known as the best, most productive plantation in Mississippi niggra or white and I am quite confident that we can do that if we all pitch in and do what we're capable of.

There will be some changes however..."

When I was finished the cheers were fewer but then I kind of expected that. Change is never easily accepted especially when things are going well but I was committed to making things being even better. I was committed to our being the best in the land which would require tireless effort. But I was as much in control of my people's destiny as the colonel was only I wasn't trying to exploit them but rather trying to implore them to be the best that they could be through education and specializing in different occupations that would make us completely autonomous and dependent on a land that was trying to take advantage of our ignorance.

"Don't feel bad honey. We are our own worst enemy but don't take it personal it's not directed towards you Andrew. It's just that they don't know any better. They've been s brainwashed into thinking that only white folks can lead them so they're really skeptical when you take the mantle and tell them what's going to happen and how they're lives are going to change in the future."

"I know Petunia and it's a shame but I can't worry about that now. We have too much work to do. I want you to get to work on the school. And send Jeremiah to see me."

"You expecting trouble Andrew?"

94

"I'm not expecting anything. I'm just planning for the unexpected," I said as I looked over the papers and the accumulated assets. There was one particular envelope that caught my attention. The envelope read Three Wind Niggras. Opening it I read Missy's plans for the slaves once they were emancipated. Her goals mirrored mine and there was a note indicating a bank account with me as a joint account holder which I would see about tomorrow.

"Andrew, my friend, how did it go?"

"A little skirmish on the way in but no one was hurt. We are now the sole owners of Three Winds."

"And by now all of Jackson knows that."

"Yes, and that's why I called you."

"I've already doubled the guard and have another platoon on standby. We have forty men standing guard and an additional twenty for tonight. Ol' Ben sent word that they hit them last night but that they fought them off."

"Any injuries?"

"One minor but a host of others on the other side. Ben said they went home whimpering like little children," Jeremiah said smiling. "Ol' Ben has established himself quite a fighting unit over there."

"Doesn't compare to ours thought does it?"

"Come my friend. With me at the helm how could it?"

It wasn't long before I was to find out. As Fiona, Petunia and Jeremiah sat down for dinner we heard a sharp burst of gunfire from the front gates. Drawing our guns we headed in that direction.

"Where's the nigga in charge of this here place?" sat a tall gentleman in a Confederate uniform.

"I'm afraid the war's over sir," I said in an attempt to appear polite. "How may I help you?"

"Oh a fancy nigga what seems to have some schoolin'. Well, that don't matter to me. A nigga's a nigga and as long as I live he ain't ownin' no land in this man's Mississippi. Do you hear me nigga?"

"Yes sir. I do hear you but I do believe there are a few friends of mine that would disagree," as I watched forty of Jeremiah's special troops dressed in all black emerge from the woods surrounding them.

"Damn nigga got an army," he said surprised to find he and his men surrounded. "No army sir. Like I said just a few of my friends."

"Well, nigga you may have caught us by surprise today but we'll be back and we'll have something for you and your friends," he said turning to leave

"We'll be here sir."

"Checkmate," Petunia said grinning. "Come on back ya goddamn peckerwood and I'll fill ya poor white ass with buckshot ya white trash," she said yelling after them.

"Petunia!" I yelled. "We must maintain our dignity and respect especially in the face of our enemy. We never want to lower ourselves to their level. If you want to say those things you say them amongst us. Do you understand?"

"Yes, daddy. Ooh, I love it when you reprimand me," she said. "Let's see how quickly we can get rid of Fiona and Jeremiah and then you can reprimand poor lil Petunia all night long," she said grinning and holding onto my arm.

"Not tonight sweetheart. I'm expecting company."

"Fiona?"

"No, those gentlemen that just left."

96

"If they weren't they certainly will after what you said."

"You really think they'd return after seeing our men in uniform? They'd have to be crazy!"

"This is the real war to them. They fought the North but they were really fighting us and Lincoln and no other man is going to end the Civil War. The real war is to keep us enslaved and no nigga gal is going to insult a southern white gentleman. So strap up. They'll be back."

Fiona and Jeremiah finished dinner and left to prepare for the potential threat.

"They saw what we had and threatened to come back so I'm going to put a hundred men in the field and keep the reserves on standby just in case and have Ben send fifty of his. If we thwart this threat we may not have to face another one."

"Come on Jeremiah. You don't believe that."

"I guess I want to. Wishful thinking on my part."

"Okay so we're ready then?"

"As ready as we'll ever be. Do you still want the girl's out there?"

"Yes they've been there from the very beginning. I think they'd be slighted if you told them no now. It is who they are. It's what they do. Don't pull any of the men from the building of the school and hospital. That must go on regardless."

"I gotcha boss."

"And if we should be attacked remember not to fire first if it comes down to that and make sure they are firmly on our landing before anyone fires. It is only trespassing if they are only on our land."

"Gotcha boss."

Returning to the parlor I sat poring over some papers and best seeing how to get seed and livestock to keep both Three Winds and its residents thriving. With Jones's General Store taking a sizeable part of our orders I decided to order direct and count out the middle man. And in time we would open our own general store with things slightly above cost with just enough of a profit to maintain the overall operation of the store. I was carried away with the thought when I was interrupted by Petunia who walked into the room and sat in the Queen Anne chair directly across from me. Sliding the chair up so we were face-to-face she kissed me before unbuckling my belt. Then lifting her dress and petticoats she eased down on me.

I gasped, my mind going blank and just like earlier we were interrupted by gunfire. Petunia let her dress fall completely now and grabbed a pair of britches and her rifle and gun belt.

Rushing behind Petunia to the sound of the gunfire I found Jeremiah's skirmish line firmly entrenched.

"How many are there?"

"Look to be forty or fifty men. Most look to be Confederate soldiers. I noticed a few Jackson residents scattered in."

"And how do we look?"

"Well with Ol' Ben's men thrown in we probably out number them three-to-one but our boys haven't really been tested up til' now. They have no idea how many of us there are but they cross onto our land they'll find out."

"Okay. Remember to shoot to maim not to kill. We don't want to make anymore southern widows and fatherless children than we have to. We just want to send home knowing that the time for enslaving niggras is over."

"Let me go and check on Fiona."

98

I left Jeremiah feeling pretty good although in a way I knew we would be tried I still hoped that it wouldn't have had to come down to needless bloodshed.

Fiona and her men were so well concealed I had a hard time locating her and were glad that I wasn't shot in approaching her lines. Finding her I found her weeping. Puzzled I'd known her to be one of my most trusted and hardened lieutenants. Give Fiona and order to execute and it was done with haste and without emotion. In fact the only I ever saw Fiona show any emotion was late night when we were in each other's company.

"What's wrong baby?"

Staring straight ahead she said nothing.

"Fiona I've seen you in worst situations than this and never seen you drop a tear. What's bothering you?" I said taking her free hand in mine.

"Oh, Andrew I'm pregnant."

This was chilling news and the second time I'd heard those words coming from a woman's lip this month. But unlike the other I knew Fiona was going to have my baby. My thoughts raced and the impending battle was no longer a concern. I was going to be a father. I was going to be a husband. The decision I had so long avoided hadn't been made by me at all.

Shots rang out.

"That's wonderful sweetheart," I said grabbing and hugging her.

"Can't wait to tell Jeremiah. I'm going to be a father."

"And Petunia, "Fiona said smiling devilishly. "I'm sure she'll be overjoyed by the news."

"And Petunia," I said thinking of her reaction when I told her especially after what had just transpired.

I could hear the sound of a bullet as it whizzed past my head. Then there was a whole volley.

"Put your head down or my son won't have a father."

She was right as the firing on their side stepped up. We had yet to fire a single round and I was quite surprised at how well disciplined we were.

"Fiona, this might be a bad time to ask but would you marry me?"

"Here they come. Hold your fire. Hold your fire. Steady. Aim." The Confederate troops were almost upon us now. I'd say no more than twenty yards away.

"Ready. Aim. Fire!" Our soldiers let loose in unison and I watched as their aim was both true and direct leaving almost half of the initial wave shot and wounded or dying.

The second command came as their men were virtually on top of us. And with a calm, cool reserve I have not seen in nary a commander Fiona gave the second command.

"Take your time boys and make 'em count. Ready. Aim. Fire!"

I watched as the remainder of their troops tumbled from their horses. The remaining survivors galloped off in a hasty retreat as we waited for them to reassemble and proceed with a second wave. But there was no second wave and we cheered our quick victory.

Jeremiah made his way over to me a wide grin on his charcoal face.

"Our boys did even better than expected," he said proudly.

"Not even a flinch thanks to their commander."

"Think they'll be back?"

"I'm almost certain they will. When is the question though? Right now they're probably just a little stunned. They're somewhere out there licking their wounds right now and trying to figure out what just happened."

"So, you think they'll be back tonight."

"I doubt it but I'd still leave these men out here in the field until tomorrow. Keep Ben's men out here but chances are they're tending to they're wounded tonight and trying to get up some more men to make another raid tomorrow night. Should be lots of talk. Send one of Josiah's boys into O'Flannery's and see what they're planning. In the meantime we'll just go about out our business as usual. By the way, did I mention the fact that I was going to be a father?"

"Get out! Well, congratulations! I know Petunia's gonna be tickled pink. She's been in love with you ever since I can remember. I guess this was always meant to be. Like fate it was inevitable."

"It's not Petunia."

"Oh my God! You don't mean to tell me it's Fiona who's pregnant?"

"Yes, my friend."

"Well, Fiona's one beautiful woman but Petunia always knew it would be her. Have you told her yet?"

"When did I have time? I just found out myself."

"Then I guess you know that attack is nothing compared to what you're about to go through when you break the news to her. Look there she is on the way up to your house now."

I best get this over with. Give me an hour or so and I'll be out to relieve you. And congratulations on a great victory my friend."

"The victory is ours Andrew."

I made sure to congratulate each and every man I passed on a great victory as I headed toward the house. Petunia was already half undressed and pulling the sheets down when I got there.

"Petunia sweetheart, I was there when you drew up the plans for your house and I watched and supervised the construction of it. So why is it that you insist on sleeping in mine when you have your own?"

"Before we were interrupted and had to run off you weren't saying that. If I remember correctly it was more like, 'Oh sweetheart you are so good to me,' or did all that gunfire rattle those beautiful thoughts from your brain. And as far as my house is concerned I told you when it was completed and you asked me if I liked it I told you there was only one thing missing and that was you. Why the sudden change of heart? You didn't used to complain."

"Fiona's pregnant with my child."

Petunia went limp, the smile suddenly fading from her face. She slumped to the side of the bed where she sat and stared at me. And the way she stared at me sent ice through my veins. The look read betrayal and I knew as emotional as she was she was doing everything in her willpower to hold it together. When she finally managed to speak I almost wished she hadn't.

"I hardly see why this presents a problem for you Andrew. You killed the last woman pregnant with your child," she said with no remorse. "And I suggest you do the same with this one or find an equally viable solution. How many years have I waited on you Andrew?" she said getting up and reaching for what I thought were her clothes. But when she turned to face me it was not her britches that she was holding but a loaded revolver. "How long have I been loyal to you Andrew? How long have I been at your   beck-and-call always on the backburner while you go about your work? I've waited patiently while you get things in order and this is how you repay me. I carried out your orders and did your dirty work. I've killed men because you told me to and this is how you repay me?

102

Well, those days are over as of tonight Andrew. Is that understood? From now on I'm calling the shots as far as we're concerned and the first shot will be right between the eyes if you don't give me the answers I'm looking for. First of all, whatever you and Fiona have is over. She can have your bastard and raise it but whatever it is you two have is done. It died tonight. I've worked too hard and too long to take a back seat any longer.

If for any reason you want to disagree I will go straight to the sheriff and tell them how you killed missy. Is that understood?"

Realizing she was quite mad I nodded in agreement. I realized that every word she said held some truth and that she would much rather take her own life than harm me in any way. But the shock of learning Fiona was pregnant had driven her to this point and I must admit I felt not only some guilt for this admission but the hurt that I caused this woman who loved me more than life itself.

Standing there pointing the gun at my head I knew there was little I could say and only prayed that she wouldn't pull the trigger.

After awhile the tense look faded and she let the gun fall from her grasp. Hitting the floor with a thud I watched as she swayed slightly. I caught her as she fainted and laid her gently on the bed before throwing the quilt over her body.

I must admit I was shaken. I had no fear of Petunia shooting me. I knew her love for me would not allow her to do that but the idea that I'd hurt to the point that she would even contemplate shooting me was almost too much for me to bear.

I was at a crossroads as to how handle Fiona's pregnancy and Petunia's petulance but for now I had more important things to think about and so once I had her nicely tucked in I set about to see how Jeremiah and the rest of the troops were holding up when Josiah and his son's came galloping in.

"That major who led the raid against us has the whole town stirred up saying he went up against an army of thousands of niggras. Says he suffered eighteen dead and another thirty something wounded. He's calling it the biggest slave uprising in the history of the country. He's got everyone in hysterics and the town's armed themselves and blockading the streets."

"That's nothing but his ego talking in defeat. He thought he was going to come in here and run roughshod over a bunch of helpless niggras. Instead he's got to go back and explain how a rag tag of misfit niggras whooped him. But as long as their blockading the town and on the defensive they shouldn't present two much of a problem. Still, I need you to stay sharp. You never know."

"Yeah, there are still a few rabble rousers runnin' around tryna stir things up and lookin' for trouble. They're trying to gather a few of the locals to launch another raid but most of the people aren't looking for any trouble."

"Good job Josiah. Why don't you go ahead home and get some rest. I'm sure the missus is worried sick about you and her boys."

"Probably right," he smiled. "That woman worries about everything. Sometimes I think the real battle's at home."

"Always is," I said patting Josiah on the shoulder.

Josiah was a good man who had grown up and worked right alongside us niggras for most of his life and who probably felt more at home among us than he did any white man.

Orphaned at six he was put under my father's charge and we grew up in the same household almost like brothers. I trusted him and he me and I watched him grow up by my side. In the last ten years or so he'd manage to eke out a meager existence for his wife and his five boys and he recognized that he and his were considered no more than poor white trash and in many instances treated worse than any niggra slave. And for this reason Josiah kept his faith in the god book and the belief that the meek would inherit the earth.

Yet, he was not one to turn the other cheek and was more inclined to lean towards an eye-for-an-eye. And when it read 'let vengeance be mine said the Lord' Josiah was quick to point out that as a servant of the good Lord he was only helping the Lord in his cause.

Often times Josiah's anger would have to be tempered by us as he was always more than ready to do the Lord's work.

"The boy's and I will be riding in at first light to keep a hands on check on that Confederate bastard who calls himself a major. Tell you what though Andrew. It's a well known fact if you cut off the head then the body will follow and Jeremiah and I or me and one of my boys can sneak in there under the cover of darkness and bring him to justice in the good Lord's name. All you gotta do is say the word Andrew."

"I believe the good book says vengeance begets vengeance or is it violence begets violence Josiah. And though we've all been through hell Josiah we are not trying to incur the Lord's wrath my brother. We simply want to do as the Jews did in ancient Egypt and be allowed to exit from our servitude and be allowed to breathe as free men. Let vengeance be the Lord's."

"I think you go to soft on them Andrew. We are disciplined and well trained. You witnessed what we did to them and we can do it again and again until they threaten us no more. But we must move now from a position and no appear to be timid or afraid."

By this time Jeremiah and Fiona were standing there listening and I turned to them but it was easy to see that they were in league with Josiah on this. Still, I could not let them jeopardize what we had all worked so hard for by going into Jackson and attempting to right the ills of two hundred years of forced servitude.

"Certainly you might act some revenge but what have you done but made the line that divides us wider. And when you kill you only leave widows and fatherless children like open wounds to fester with a growing hatred for you and yours for years to come but even more immediately your acts though they may be immediate and victorious will not be tolerated and will eventually summon the state militia and ultimately the federal government. I don't think any of us want that. Fiona how are we on ammunition. "

"Low Andrew. One maybe two more clashes and we're out."

"And you want to antagonize them Josiah. We can't afford to do that my brother."

"I just believe that if you cut off the head you can diffuse the whole situation. Just seems smarter than sitting back at their mercy."

"We'll talk about this later Josiah. Right now I need you to grab two buckboards and a couple of hands and head to Vicksburg and buy all the ammunition you can get your hands on so we can shore up our defenses in the interim. And be hasty man. Lives depend on it."

"I'm on it," Josiah said calling two of his sons.

"Where's Petunia?"

"Sleeping I suppose. Told her you were pregnant. She didn't take the news very well."

"I'm going to go check on her," Petunia said standing to leave.

"Don't know if you want to do that. She pulled her revolver and threatened me before she fainted."

"She'll be angry but she'll get over it. Besides we need her Andrew."

"Okay but be careful Fiona," I warned.

"Never you mind. I know Petunia perhaps better than anyone and she'll bounce back. She's strong and she's committed to our cause."

"Let me know how she's doing and don't you put you or my baby at any risk Fiona."

Walking the skirmish line I found the troops well concealed and in good spirits. Many of these men I'd known for the better part of my life and felt the burden of leading these men into unchartered waters. There was a good chance that some would be killed and the burden rested on my shoulders.

At times I would hunker down with a few in their little fox holes and talk and get for these men and the mission at hand. I found most in good spirits and committed to our efforts and willing to give up their lives than be forced back into servitude of any kind.

Freedom had served most well and the idea of raising their families on their own land was most compelling and they were driven to make a success of it. I left feeling relieved and less burdened knowing now that they were most adamant about preserving the freedom they had come to know in so little time.

By the time I reached Jeremiah I was feeling much better.

"You know Andrew there is something to what Josiah was saying. That major is the primary cause of all this ruckus. I know you're all for preserving peace and saving lives but if we were to assassinate him we would be sending a message and folks would think twice about the niggras at Three Winds."

I ignored this.

"Have the men eaten?"

"No, not that I know of."

"Okay. They seem to be in pretty good spirits. I round up some grub and send it down to them," I said walking away.

"Did you hear what I said Andrew?"

"I heard you Jeremiah."

Perhaps he and Josiah were right but assassinating the major would be an act of aggression and that I did not want. Let them be the aggressors. With the casualties they'd already taken an assassination attempt would only lead insult to injury like kicking a man when he was down and out.

No let them smart over the loss they'd already taken and then decide if they wanted more. But there would be no provocation on our part. None whatsoever. If they attack us at Three Winds we at least had a right to defend ourselves although niggras still had no rights under the law. But should any of us get caught trying to assassinate a confederate war hero in Jackson and that meant a lynching for sure.

Entering the house I was pleased to find Fiona and Petunia in the kitchen engaged in a rather joyful banter.

"I'm just waiting til you blow up heifer. He surely won't want you looking like a full blown sow. Then I'll take over where you left off and train him to be more selective when looking for a woman. Right now he don't know the difference between a wild boar and a full-blooded mulattoe queen. That's why your nappy-headed African ass is pregnant."

"I'm pregnant because there's love between us. He's only with you when I'm busy. And when he lays down with you and closes his eyes ask him who he sees. It's me Petunia. Me. The only reason he sleeps with you at all is because he feels sorry for you

and he's a good and charitable man. He told me you're no more than a charity fuck and asked me if it was okay. I told him to go ahead and give to the less fortunate that can't get a man to sleep with them."

I smiled and made my way up to the bedroom after suggesting that they may wanna feed the troops.

I was awakened to gunfire in the wee hours of the morning and looking out of the second story window I was able to see a continuous flash of muzzle fire coming from what appeared to be the front gates of Three Winds. Grabbing my field glasses I peered out again. From what I gathered there had to be close to a hundred rifles firing but there was no return fire.

Fiona, who had been curled up on one side of me grabbed her clothes and rifle. And Petunia who was at the foot of the bed quickly did the same. I continued to watch. There was a concerted shelling for close to twenty minutes and still no return fire from Three Winds.

108

Dressing quickly I made my way to the front lines to find Josiah handing out rounds of cartridges to the men as the men calmly awaited instruction. There were no hasty charges from the major or his men this time and bullets whizzed all around but being that my men had months to choose their positions and were well entrenched they were hardly in any danger. Meanwhile Jeremiah and Josiah's sniper units which had a

clear view of the front gates stood ready to inflict hurt on any one who crossed over onto Three Winds. Every now and then some overly eager member of the major's brigade would come galloping in shouting some obscenity in trying to make a name for himself would scream out in pain as a bullet from the trees or one of the snipers strongholds would pluck him off his horse gut shot and writhing in the dust. As morning approached things died down and I knew they were waiting for dawn to mount a charge. Moving closer I could see that there close to a hundred men—some ex confederate soldiers and a good many civilians just milling around in small groups.

With the numbers they had I knew they were intent on driving us back, scattering us and picking us off one-by-one. There was a good chance they could and so I abandoned my plan and told Jeremiah to have his snipers at the ready. Then grabbing Fiona, Petunia and Ol' Ben's units which had seen considerable raids over the years as part of the council I flanked the major's forces and lit into them in unison with a concerted effort.

Concentrated rifle fire chopped down a good twenty to twenty five men initially and when the major called for a retreat Petunia's men lay in waiting and with a blistering barrage halted the retreating troops in their tracks. With nowhere to go the major burrowed in and the remaining troops put up a gallant fight until late in the afternoon.

Because of our familiarity with the terrain and expert marksmanship surrender by the major's now surrounded forces now seemed inevitable and each time one of the major's men would show himself one of Jeremiah or Josiah's snipers would inevitably pick him off. Alas and down to no more than thirty men the major finally threw up the white flag of surrender.

Josiah and his son's were always our front and went out to meet the major.

"Don't care how it appears I know you're working for that niggra. You're a traitor to your race sir."

"I'm not here to discuss my affiliations with you major but simply to arrange for the terms of your surrender. We will let your men go and you sir will be tried by our tribunal on terms of trespassing and assault on a civilian population which equates to crimes against humanity. Do you agree to the terms of surrender or will you stand by and watch the total elimination of the remainder of your forces?"

"I will agree to your terms of your surrender?"

"Then I will accompany you back to your camp and arrange for the release of the rest of your men."

"Very well sir."

Weapons confiscated and with the release of his men along with the wounded and dead bodies the remainder of the major's forces limped woefully back towards Jackson escorted by twenty five or so of our troops as armed escorts.

The major himself sat high atop his horse. Shackled he was quickly led through our troops who cheered our victory on his way to the place where we had long ago held our council meetings.

When all was said only our senior council members were there and the only member not from Three Winds was Ol' Ben."

"This tribunal is being called today on August 24, 1870 in light of certain crimes against humanity perpetrated by Major G. London Foley against the civilian population of Three Winds Plantation on August 23rd and August 24th in the year of our Lord 1870. How does the defendant plead? The defendant pleads guilty. All in favor of this guilty plea please raise your hands. By a jury of his superiors we find the defendant guilty by a unanimous vote and sentence him to hang by the neck until dead. The sentence will be carried out at once."

"What the hell?" the major shouted. "Do you niggas know who I am? I am Major G. London Foley. I served under General Jefferson Davis and was decorated for my service at both Bull Run and Chickamauga."

"And perhaps that's where you should have ended your career major. The war is over. Perhaps you should have accepted defeat more gracefully. String him up boys."

I had had enough of death and dying and turned and walked away leaving the honors to Ol' Ben and Jeremiah who made haste with his sentencing.

On the way back to the house most of the folks were celebrating and after relieving most of the troops and leaving a skeletal crew of about forty for security we joined in on the festivities as well.

I left both Petunia and Fiona on duty that night much to their chagrin determined to get a good night's rest but no sooner had I fallen into a much needed sleep. I was exhausted there was the sound I dreaded so much. Rushing half dressed outside I turned to the sound of the gunfire which I was surprised to find was coming from the west. I was not the only one rushing and I soon bumped into Fiona.

"They surprised us and hit us from the West Fork. We had about fifteen soldiers guarding the West Fork and we're holding but just barely. It's a two pronged attack this time meant to split us. As soon as I got my people over there Petunia sent word that they were attacking from the front as well."

"How many men do we have available?"

"About thirty total? Everyone else was sent home."

"Did you send someone out to mobilize the rest?"

"Yeah. And I believe Jeremiah's doing the same. I sent Josiah over to summon Ben. Doesn't seem to be more than twenty or so from the west and from what I'm getting from Petunia maybe another twenty or so at the main gate. Right now we're holding our own. They just caught us by surprise is all."

111

"I'm tired Fiona. Let's wipe this hatred from the face of the earth once and for all."

"Gather yourself Andrew. Even Jesus had to fight for his kingdom. And it wasn't easy. It was one long continuous battle. You couldn't have possibly believed that the devil was going to put up token resistance when your aim is to do good. Now gather yourself man and assemble your unit so we can drive them back to hell they came from."

I turned to face many of my men standing idly by waiting for my instruction.

"Join in," I said to them pointing to the foxholes already occupied by Fiona's unit. "Don't fire unless you have them fixed firmly within your sights. And then keep firing until there's not a one left." I said before dashing off to see how the rest of the troops were faring.

Coming into a clearing I was relieved to see Jeremiah and Josiah standing on a high bluff overlooking the battle from both sides.

"How we doing?" I asked hoping for some better news.

"Don't think they're going to let this thing die easily, Andrew." Jeremiah said lighting his pipe. "Perhaps it was a mistake accepting their surrender and having the mercy to let them go. All they did was go back and reassemble. I see some of those same ones right back here again."

"Well this time there will be no mercy!" I said.

"I don't know who the young lieutenant is but he seems a lot more organized than the major was and it looks like they have a steady flow of people joining him."

"That would be his son," Josiah said as he came riding up.

"So, I guess instead of dissolving things by taking the major we only inflamed the situation. We've made him a martyr."

"I guess I'm to blame for that," Josiah said dropping his head in shame.

112

"We are all to blame for that," Jeremiah said.

"There is no time to place blame. We have a battle to win."

"Ol' Ben is here. He wants to know where you want him."

"The lieutenant looks as if he's splitting his troops again. From what I can see it looks like he's sending through the woods and trying to flank my unit." Petunia said as she joined us.

"You have a detachment in the woods?"

Petunia smiled.

"You know I do. Maybe fifteen or twenty from Jeremiah's unit plus another four or five snipers in the trees. We were going to flank him and were just waiting on your word."

"So they're walking into an ambush and I need to be there."

"No. You want to be there so you can take all the glory." Petunia said grinning.

Jeremiah grinned back and made his way to the tree lined grove not far away.

"So, how are we doing overall?"

"Well, they caught us totally by surprise this time and so we took some casualties but we regrouped and put up a pretty good front and held them off. I think we're ready to make a push but I didn't want to advance without your word cause if we do we're going to take some hits."

"That's all part of war Petunia and you know that. You're going to have to learn to make that call."

"I know Andrew. But it doesn't make it easy," she said dropping her head.

"Ain't nothin' about war easy Petunia. But I shouldn't have to carry the weight of the world on my head when I have good lieutenants."

"I hear you."

I turned away from her and hugged my good friend Ben.

"Sorry to have had to call you back so soon Ben."

"Your fight has always been my fight. And until we eliminate the enemy once and for all it will always be our fight."

I hugged my father's best friend again.

"How many men do you have Ben?"

"Four units. A little over a hundred and twenty men. Oh, and six or seven nurses just in case."

"Good. Good. From what I see they have close to two hundred men and it looks like more are dwindling in all the time."

"So, this is it?"

"Looks that way."

"You know I'm an old man now and lived a full life. But you know you don't get old being no fool. And the minute I heard Josiah say we needed to assassinate that there major I knew we were stirring up a hornet's nest. Assassinating him was no more than a call to arms."

"I know Ben. But you couldn't tell them that. Now all we can do is defend what's ours."

"That's all we can do. We're do you want my men?"

"Well, let's see if we can end this before we have every confederate rebel in the state breathing down our necks. The majority of their forces are at the front gate so send three units up there and tell Petunia to advance when

114

they get there. And this time there will be no prisoners and no surrender. Show no mercy.

The rest you can send to Fiona who's over on the west gate. I'm not too worried about her though. That gal can hold her own."

Ol' Ben chuckled.

"You can tell you two share the same genes," he said before wheeling the young black stallion off towards his men.

I was glad to have Ol' Ben's support but his words puzzled me. Still, there was no time to think about that now and I moved up to Petunia's unit which had tripled in size thanks to Ben.

"Andrew with the way they're laying down fire I cannot in good faith order my men to charge. That's suicide."

Now laying beside her and feeling the steady fire I knew she was right.

"I'm going to take a handful of men and set up a diversion on their flank to draw their fire. Once I draw their fire you advance but use your good sense and do it with extreme caution."

"Gotcha."

I slipped away and summoned fifteen or twenty men and set up a line some thirty or forty feet away and began blistering them with fire until we had all their attention. They were close enough to hear me when I yelled.

"Fix bayonets."

And I could see several of their men tuck tail and run at the sound of my command thinking they were about to be overrun by a superior force but the superior force was not us and minutes later they met with Petunia's men who were no match when it came to hand-to-hand combat. Already engaged with Petunia's men my unit of twenty or so men hit them and tilted the odds even more in our favor and the rout was on.

They executed a hasty retreat and we formed intermittent skirmish lines firing steadily at the fleeing troops all but wiping them out. But these were fighting men and those that did escape joined the men at the west gate and when we arrived Fiona was barely hanging on under a steady barrage of gunfire and mounting casualties.

Petunia fell down in the foxhole alongside of Fiona as bullets whizzed past their heads.

"Goodness gal. I woulda though you woulda had this all taken care of by now. Me and my unit done sent them ol' confederate boys runnin'. I done took Andrew up to the house cooked, ate, fed him and bedded him down and you still out here playin' wit' these fools.

To tell you the truth I was gettin' a lil bored after lovin' Andrew so I said let me go find my girl and see if she wanna play some Gin Rummy and Jeremiah tells me you still out here tryna fight off these white boys. I couldn't believe it. But I figured just like everything else I'd best come down here and show you how it's done so wala here I is," Petunia said grinning before reloading and squeezing off another round.

"These ain't your usual shoot 'em and watch 'em run white boys Petunia. We gotta different breed than what you're used to. You shoot one of these peckerwoods in the ass and they turn and look at you and say, 'is that all you got?' No. These here are of the belligerent nature."

"Well, I'm getting a little tired so let me go head and put an end to this."

"You do that gal!" Fiona said winking at her girl.

Petunia slid out of the foxhole on her belly and once out of range stood up and summoned her unit around her.

"Just like we did upfront boys… While Fiona's unit keeps 'em occupied we're going to flank them on both sides and hit 'em hard. You got me?"

Everyone nodded in agreement.

"Any questions?"

116

"No ma'am, they shouted in unison.

"Then let's whoop some rebel tail tonight!"

Ol' Ben said it was like Petunia had a suicide wish as she led the charge

down on the West Fork with rifles blazing she went into the tree line
screaming some passages from Revelations and after twenty or twenty five
minutes there was no rebel fire to speak of as she over rode their position
and then doubled back making short work of the dying and wounded. Ben
said it was like she was a woman possessed and not the Petunia he'd come
to know.

I worried about Petunia after hearing the same thing from a few of my
other lieutenants and it bothered me some that Petunia who had no
penchant for firing a weapon let alone leading a raid had suddenly become
so gung ho for lack of a better word but there was no time to sit and reflect
on her sudden metamorphosis.

This time there were no festivities or celebrations following our victory
and the only ones who were allowed to move from their positions were the
burial crews.

In all we counted eighty four dead confederate soldiers and fourteen of our
own. And though many saw it as an overwhelming victory but to me one
death was a resounding loss.

We stayed hunkered down in our foxholes careful not to be surprised
again for two days and it wasn't until the sheriff and judge came riding in
to tell us that the men responsible for the attacks on Three Winds were
being held and tried and would pay some healthy fines for this melee. But
we were banned from coming into Jackson for the foreseeable future
because of all the death and pain we had brought to the residents of
Jackson.

At this point Josiah had both the sheriff and the judge follow him to the
fourteen graves of the soldiers so they could see those that had been killed
by those unprovoked attacks.

In the end the council agreed that it was something that had to be done, something that needed to be done almost like a purging and now perhaps we could start over.

When they'd left we returned to our lives and security was returned to the forty or so men who usually stood guard over Three Winds and retired to our homes exhausted but with a much greater appreciation for what we had and the fact that we would defend with our lives that which was ours but more importantly our freedom.

To say that I was tired would be an understatement and the hard part had only just begun. Fiona, Ben. Jeremiah and Petunia made our rounds to the homes of the fallen soldiers and this may have very well been the hardest thing I'd ever done in my life. Many of these boys I'd known, grown up with, and worked with over the years.

Some were friends. They were fathers, brothers, sons and the like. Overall it was a sobering affair and one that I hope to God I may never have to do again. And I couldn't wait to simply lay down with Fiona and my baby and hold her and have the security of my family close to my bosom. And yet there was something that Ol' Ben had sad in passin' that had been gnawing at me since he'd said it.

Agreeing to meet by the old oak when everyone was finished Jeremiah and I sat quietly puffing on our corncob pipes just as we'd done as boys until Fiona, Petunia and Ben joined us. They'd all looked as if they'd seen better days and they all sat in a somewhat comfortable silence.

"War and killing is always an ugly business but depending on what you're fighting for it can have some deeply satisfying results and perhaps you had to go through this so you can move ahead and progress and appreciate the gifts that have been bestowed upon us." Ben said.

"That's very true Ben," Jeremiah said shaking his head in agreement.

And again there was silence.

"Ben can I ask you something about something you mentioned when we were over on the west fork when you were referring to Fiona."

"Sure boy. You know you can ask me anything?"

"Well, when Fiona had her troops laying down fire on those rebs you said you didn't expect anything less being that she bore the same genes. I'm not sure I understand. Explain what you meant."

"Well sometimes when you get old you speak when you shouldn't and I guess that was one of those times Andrew."

"Please finish Ben."

"Oh, I suppose it can't hurt now. You see when your father was a young man he was a lot like you. He was bright, intelligent and he saw things. He had a plan. He was a lot like you. He had a vision. And people noticed. The women noticed and they were all attracted to him, vying for his attention and most of the time he brushed them off. But there were two women in particular that caught his eye. One was your mother and the other was a beautiful African girl named Sally Mae.

Now your mother was from the old country and had certain traditions and at first pretended she had no interest in your father and it wasn't until she got wind of Sally Mae also having an interest in your father that she even considered him. By that time, your father being a man of action had impregnated Sally Mae. And lo and behold she had a daughter. Well, your father being the man he was insisted on telling your mother who was vehemently opposed to having this daughter in her house. So, your father paid Aunt Bessie to take care of the little girl so he could keep his child close to him. That daughter was Fiona, your sister and that's why I made the comment that you share the same genes. But I'm quite sure you've heard that story before.

I hadn't and I was devastated to say the least. Fiona who sat across from me stared at the ground and the silence was deafening.

"Tell me you two didn't know?"

"No," was also I could venture to say.

"Well, perhaps I've said too much. They say with age comes wisdom. Sometimes I'm afraid that isn't always the case. And with that said I guess this is as good a time as any to make my leave."

"Just a minute Ben but do you mind if I have a word with you in private," Fiona said the tears flowing down her face. The two walked over to Ben's mule and I watched as Fiona slumped not once but twice as Ben held her upright in his arms and summoned Jeremiah with his free hand to come and get the distraught woman. Jeremiah rose quickly and went to assist the old man with the young woman.

"He's my brother Jeremiah. My brother…"

"How were you to know Fiona? This comes as much as a surprise to us as to you."

"I understand that but I am in love with my brother. I am pregnant by my brother. It's an abomination, a sin in the eyes of God."

"The God I know is a forgiving God and he cannot will not hasten to judge you on things out of your control."

"I cannot stay here Jeremiah. Would you tell Andrew for me? Make him know how sorry I am. Tonight I will gather up my things and will be out of here by first light."

"I will tell him Fiona if that's what you want but in time this too shall pass. You are as much a part of my family as Andrew and Petunia and I would hate for you to leave. We have come so far and it would be sad to see you go especially at the time of our greatest victory."

"I can't see how I could stay Jeremiah with my being in love and sleeping with my brother for years. What will folks say?"

"I could take you as my wife Fiona and I wish someone would utter a word about my wife and my child."

"But we don't love each other in that way Jeremiah."

120

"I have always loved you Fiona but would never step on my brother's toes."

"You're just saying that Jeremiah."

"We will tell them tomorrow."

"You would do that for me Jeremiah?"

"It is done."

"Let's tell Andrew and Petunia."

That night we all celebrated and I guess the news from Ol' Ben was still a shock as I drank far too much and Jeremiah and Petunia had to carry me too bed. The news of Jeremiah and Fiona's marriage also came as a shock and I knew that Jeremiah who valued his freedom as much as any man was only making this sacrifice to aid Fiona's shame and embarrassment.

I felt Jeremiah's love and commitment to holding our family together and knew that after all we'd been through Three Winds would forever be strong.

And for some reason Petunia seemed even happier than usual.

Part Three

Jeremiah and Fiona were married the following Sunday and all of Three Winds attended as did Ol' Ben's folks from over at the O'Reilly Place and a host of others from the other plantations in league with the council. I was a glorious time and for the first time since I'd known him Jeremiah truly looked happy. And though Fiona still could not face me she too appeared if not happy at least content and at peace.

And let me not forget petunia who was absolutely ecstatic and couldn't do enough to help her friend adjust to her new role as wife and mother to be knitting and speaking of the baby as if it were her own.

More than anything she now thought of herself as the first lady of Three Winds and although she never said a word to that affect she certainly outdid any southern white woman I'd ever seen in the role. There wasn't a day there wasn't a day there wasn't some white woman pulling up with a trunk load of dresses straight from Boston or New Orleans. There was not a day that Petunia did not don a different outfit to parade around Three Winds in her brand new carriage. Little was said as most of the inhabitants of Three Winds were quite prosperous as well. And all looked at Petunia as a symbol of our prosperity and knew that they weren't far away from embodying what Petunia had ascribed to. She made her daily rounds meeting with all her old friends and cohorts but was never smug or pretentious remaining the same old lively, mischievous Petunia with a smart mouth and an easy manner whether smoking her corn cob pipe with the field hands or talking to the ladies.

And aside from her dress I saw little difference as she continually prompted me when it came to the topic of marriage. Summarily, I did as I'd always done and dismissed her matter-of-factly.

"Lincoln married Mary Todd not knowing she had mental issues but I am aware that there is something very wrong with you and even if there weren't I have no plans of marrying so why must you continually persist asking me something that I am not apt to do.

You are far too feeble minded for me to even entertain such a course of action. And if I were to ever consider marriage you would be the last woman on God's green earth that I would consider marrying,"

Now there was not much if anything that would or could upset Petunia but if something could it was my constant refusal to marry her. And never have you seen a woman fly off the handle as she would but fly off the handle she would throwing the fine China she'd had imported all the way from England. It would tickle me and I never saw her penchant for marriage when we were living as such anyway. Most of the time though she would sit in the reading room and while away her time away reading and then burst through the doors of my study to announce some phenomenal event that she'd just read about and tell me how her children—those were her students—which would fill the classroom at her school would love this story or that.

That was her other passion. The school was only a month or so from being completed. And as yet she hadn't hired a teacher. Oh she'd brought in a host of candidates to fill the three open spots. But out of the twenty or thirty applicants she'd interviewed thus far not a one had close to meeting her standards. Either they weren't caring or compassionate enough or they didn't have the academic know how to take her kids where she wanted them to go.

It all tickled me and as opening date was just around the way I chuckled as her anxiety grew I watched as she cussed and fussed.

"Petunia why don't you just hire someone on an interim basis until you find a suitable teacher and then replace them?"

"I should have hired that lil' ol' niggra woman that came all the way from Massachusetts. I was just so afraid that the children wouldn't be able to relate to her if she didn't pass out and die in front of the class. That woman had to be close to ninety and when she pulled out the brown jug during the interview and started sipping from it I said oh hell no. And to think that was the best of the lot."

"Or perhaps you could have hired the elderly niggra man that believed that all the education a niggra needed was to be able to put his mark on a piece of paper and count straw to match how many cows one had."

"See what I'm saying Andrew?"

"Why don't you hire Ben? His mere presence commands respect and he's not only learned but a plethora of knowledge as well. I think he'd do very well with the older children."

"And he's exactly what we need—some older men with a commanding presence. Do you think he'd do it?"

"Only one way to find out."

"That's a splendid idea. And you could do the third class Andrew. Oh why didn't I think of that. Here I am searching all ove creation and I'm sitting on a gold mine right here."

"Whoa. Whoa. Whoa sweetie. Don't go jumping the gun. There's no way I could do that with the blacksmithing class I already have in addition to running the blacksmith shop. I can hardly handle what I have already."

"Oh come on Andrew. You'd be perfect. And you're always talking about Justice being as good if not better than you at nineteen. Let him train your class. He can do that but he can't teach and you're so patient with children. And I'm pretty sure you can offer them a little more than putting their mark on a paper and using straws to count cows. You can take the little ones and they'll only be in school a half a day. You'll be finished by noon and have the rest of the day to tend to your business."

"Woman you're going to be the death of me."

A week or two later Ben and I stood outside the three room school house and marveled at the structure which stood handsomely with its marble pillars and large sunlit classrooms. I had to admit it was a fine structure and one that rival any in the state as far as I knew.

Across from it stood a similarly elegant structure although somewhat smaller in size. In it housed the Three Winds Memorial Hospital. And two doors down from it was the new general store which was still under construction. All in all, Three Winds was becoming a town unto itself. Nearly autonomous there now was hardly a need to leave the premises.

Each weekend Three Winds residence brought their goods to market and bought and bartered amongst themselves in what was as much a social gathering as an exchange of goods.

"Things are good here for you my friend," Ben said to me outside of school one morning.

"They're getting there," I replied.

"Many a day I have thought about coming to Three Winds to live."

"And we would welcome you. You know that."

"I do but then not only am I too old to move but we are in far worse shape than you and my folks have no one to look after them. The night riders still come through

126

with their white hoods on wreaking havoc amongst my people and we have all we can do to hold them off. I'm afraid if there wasn't a chapter of the council there they wouldn't have survived."

"And why wasn't I informed Ben?"

"Well, to be quite frank you've had your hands quite full here at Three Winds with your own battles. What we have are mere skirmishes."

"And how long has this been going on?"

"Bout the same time things ended here. They haven't done anything but changed their focus. They know they can't do anything at Three Winds and fare they'll meet less resistance with us so they've been trying to burn us out and lay fire to our crops. That sort of thing; just harassing us is all. We fight 'em off but usually not before they've caused considerable damage. It's nothing you can set up a defense for. We have standing guards but they sneak through our lines and pour kerosene all over the crops, light fire to them and while we're tending to the fire they'll set fire to a barn or someone's hut. That sort of thing."

"Have you caught any of them?"

"No. Like I said they sneak in and out."

"And you met with the council surrounding this matter?"

"Just our council."

"And?"

"Nothing more than to keep fending them off like we've been doing."

"And how's that working for you so far?"

"Hasn't been. If anything the raids have increased."

"Okay soon as we're finished with class I'm going to hold an emergency meeting of the council. I think I have a plan that will nip these raids in the bud. But for now send word to your place o double the guard around the clock but our aim is not to kill or hurt anyone but to capture one of these night riders."

"I'll send word now."

"Remember we need one held captive."

Later that evening as I sat home pouring over books trying to find something my children's attention for tomorrow's class I wondered if Josiah had had any success when I heard the sound of a horse approaching.

"Were you able to see the judge?"

"Yeah. I saw him and it's just as you said Andrew. We ain't got no rights under the laws of Mississippi. A white man has the right to ride onto your land and destroy

your land and kill your children but you do not have the right to defend yourself under the law. Any violent retaliation upon a white man and the sentence is hanging."

"I was pretty sure that's how it was but thanks for confirming that for me Josiah."

"Even if a niggra did have the right to defend his land Ol' Ben still wouldn't be within his jurisdiction to defend his land because he doesn't own the land. The O'Reilly land is under the jurisdiction of the Freedmen's bureau and hasn't been outwardly awarded to them as of yet."

"Right you are again Josiah. Which means there's only one course of action left to us."

"And that is?"

"To be covert and use similar tactics. The worst thing you can do is steal from a thief. And the worst thing we can do is to hit them at home with similar raids and who better to do that than the council."

"And I think that after everything we've been through I should be permitted to join the council on these raids."

"Not with a wife and five sons Josiah."

"Is that it Andrew or is it because the council by-laws prevent whites from joining?"

"I have never looked at you as anything but my brother Josiah and you know that. Perhaps the by-laws should have been changed years ago if for no other reason than to have admitted you but I can't allow you to put yourself in jeopardy. Rose and the boys depend on you."

"I suppose."

"Send Jeremiah if you pass by the west fork on your way home. Be subtle. I don't want Fiona involved."

"I'll do that."

An hour or two later Jeremiah arrived and we sat down and went over the plans. I sent close to seventy five men over to Ben's to stand guard and canvas the place. There were no gaps in the perimeter now so anyone trying to step foot onto the place would immediately be apprehended. It was now just a matter of time until the trap was sprung.

Two days late a crier came tearing into Three Winds.

"Master Andrew! Master Andrew! Master Ben sent me! He wants you to come at once!"

"Do you need me to go with you?" Petunia asked her concern obvious.

"No," I said trying to console her and waylay any worry on her part. "It's just a small council matter that needs resolved."

"You sure?" She asked. She'd known me far too long to know that it was more than a mere council meeting.

"I'll be fine," I said kissing her on the cheek. "Be back before the turkey's done," I said smiling.

Pulling the young boy up onto the back of the horse and lighting out at a quick gallop my thoughts went back to Petunia. In the last month or so she had been softer, calmer, more reserved. At first I thought it was simply the fact that Fiona was no longer in the picture coupled with the fact that the school was up and running and she was teaching and had seemingly found her niche. Her idle time she spent reading and all in all seemed quite content with her new lifestyle. But her overly concern about my well-being was something new and was beginning to weigh on me.

Arriving at the O'Reilly Place minutes later I met with Ben who embraced me warmly and asked me to follow him. I did so and prior to entering the barn where three or four other council members stood guard I was handed a black hood which I promptly donned as did Ben before entering.

Inside I was surprised to find not one but two relatively young southern white gentlemen in their mid-twenties.

"These two gentlemen were caught trying to set fire to the barn killing the livestock and the stores of crops for the winter. Under the council's system of justice these are offenses clearly punishable by death. I don't believe there is any real need for them to stand trial. Is there any need to take a vote or should we just get on with sentencing?"

"Hang the bastards and leave the bodies in the road for all to see," someone yelled.

"Is there anyone who is opposed?"

Not a sound was heard in either of the men's defense.

"Then the only question left to answer is the way in which they die."

"An eye for an eye is what the good book teaches us," I said.

"Then let them burn."

It was all rather quick and the two men were then led away. It was growing dark now as evening was suddenly upon us and though a steady stream of tears rolled down the younger man's face the older remained stoic and resolved in his fate.

I walked alongside the younger one sensing some remorse now that he was facing a most painful end.

"Why son? Why would you set fire to the crops and the animals? You know that those people depend on those to live."

"They told me to do it sir. I didn't want to do it but they told me to do it. It wasn't like I had a choice."

"But you did have a choice son. Now you have to face the punishment for your crimes."

Faced with a most gruesome death the boy hung his head and let out a wail that could echoed among the forest.

"Shut up lil' brother. Have some honor and dignity as a Confederate soldier."

"Do not listen to him. There is no war. There is no confederacy. And there is no honor in burning the crops of men who toil long hours in the fields to feed their yonguns. Where is the honor in that? Where is the honor of smelling your own flesh burn for stealing food from the mouths of others and raiding and shooting innocent people in the middle of the night? Where is the honor in wearing hoods and doing the devil's work?"

The young man was more than remorseful as the council members placed enough brush around a young oak and then tied the older of the two men to the tree before dousing the branches and kindling with kerosene.

Ben took the blindfolds off both men.

"You fuckin' niggas will burn in hell for this," the man bound to the tree yelled.

131

Ben and the rest of the council members sat in a small half circle in front of the tree as the man hurled expletive after expletive cursing us for being niggas and the very scourge of the earth.

"How can one man have so much hate in him for a people he has never met or known?" Ben turned to me and asked.

"You are much older and wiser than I my friend. I gave up asking why a long time ago."

"It don't mean nothin'. It's just the way we was brought up," the young man said. "We was just brought up to hate niggas. It ain't nothin' personal. It's just the way it is here in the South."

"I think you're mistaken son. I think it means somethin' to the mama and daddy of that niggra hangin' from some tree. Just like you and your brother's burnin' is gonna mean somethin' to your mama and daddy when they receive the charred remains of your bodies."

"And then what? Then we come back and kill one of you'ns?"

"I suppose. But then you're killing us for no apparent reason and I guess we're supposed to just say thank you Mr. White Man for killing and burning my peoples. Sorry son but those days are long gone. Set the torch Ben!"

The flames burst into a furious fire and the older brothers expletives were now little more than screams of pain and just as quickly as they began they ended. The young man who sat next to me now wept openly for his older brother.

"Each time you raid our villages and lynch a niggra this is how we feel," I remarked to him. "I take no pleasure in killing any man but we will not sit back and be victimized by you White folks any longer. As I said those days are long past. But we are a merciful people and I will let you go to take your brothers remains home with your

word that you will do your part to end the carnage of my people and yours. Is that understood? Or you can meet the same fate as your brother."

132

The younger man looked at me.

"Like I said sir, I ain't neva wanted to do this in the first place. They sent me and told me I had to."

"I believe you son which is why I'm sparing your life. Now make it your life's work to change this evilness. Make it your passion to end the ceaseless carnage and cruelty to others. Teach your children that it's wrong to hate and perhaps we can start building a better world. I'm counting on you son. And know that each time you encounter this or something like this towards niggras or white folks know that you have a responsibility to help end this hatred between our peoples. Remember that the only reason you are alive is because a niggra, a descendant of Abraham and Moses showed you mercy. Now gather up your brothers remains and get outta here. Ben can you have someone hook up the buckboard so this boy can take the remains of his brother home?"

Blindfolded we led the boy out of the woods and once on the main road leading towards Jackson we took the blindfold off and gave him the reins. With a five minute head start we then followed at a safe distance. Then were eight of us in the party all council members and although we had sent a clear message our mission had only just begun.

The boy made rapid haste and then turned off onto a dusty patch of road not more than five miles from the Jackson city limits. The road was narrow and from the underbrush which sprouted up everywhere it was clear that it was a road not readily used. So narrow was it that it made it hard for the buckboard and slowed the young man's journey considerably. Several times we came close to overtaking him and being found out when alas it widened and opened into a beautiful apple orchard and then into a clearing where sat a most modest home. Not a hundred yards away a long bunk house and next to that a good size barn. A large pasture sat off to the right of the house and if I were to venture to guess I would say there were no less than a hundred or so cows grazing peacefully.

Ben and a few of the boys hid in the tree lines while others went about the task of dousing the barn and bunkhouse with kerosene.

"Is everybody in position?" I whispered. "Torch the barn!"

133

I watched as the young man came from the house. His mother was wailing but his old man and brothers showed little or no emotion as they removed the charred remains from the buckboard.

Six or seven men stood outside the door of the bunkhouse watching the grieving family but only one or two approached to offer any sort of condolences when the father

said 'Let's ride boys!' much to the chagrin of the mother and the young man I had just freed.

"Father! This killing must stop!"

"Move out of the way fool," the old man said shoving his son to the ground. "You were always the weak one. Do you see what those heathen niggas did to your brother?" he screamed. "Now if you've got any sand in ya mount up. We're gonna kill us some niggas tonight."

"But father…"

No sooner had the boy said that then the barn burst into flames followed by the adjoining bunkhouse. And as the remaining men made their way out, some in just their pajamas I ordered Ben's snipers to fire. They were even deadlier and precise than they'd been some months earlier and every time a shot went off a man fell until the only one's standing was the old man, the boy and his mother.

"I showed compassion in sparing your son's life so he could tell you that this killing must come to an end but you would not listen to your boy who it seems is far wiser than you. Now instead of having six sons you only have one. And there is no one to blame for their deaths but you. I burned your barn to show you how it feels when a man works all his life to build just to have someone come along and take it just because. And still I can see the embers of hatred burning in your eyes. My father used to tell me

that all men are not meant to live," I said raising the gun and pointing it right between his eyes and squeezing the trigger. The gun did not go off. The man smiled.

"You're going to have to do better than that if you plan on killing me nigga," he chuckled.

"Father!"

But it was too late. I squeezed the trigger again. This time the gun did go off and I watched as the man fell at my feet.

The young man's tears flowed freely as he sought to console his mother who was beyond distraught.

"Oh my God! My boys! My beautiful boys!" she said moving from one son's body to the next. I watched as she moved grief-stricken and inconsolable into the house followed by her son.

As I turned the big bay horse around I heard the scream door slam and the young man's voice.

"No mother! This must stop. It must end here!"

Before I could turn again to see what all the commotion was about I felt a deep burning fire in my shoulder and found myself laying on my backside looking up at Ben who was taking careful aim. Despite the pain in my shoulder and saw the boy's mother

reloading the shotgun but before she could squeeze off another round the bullet from Ben's rifle slammed into her already frail chest lifting her off the ground and slamming into the wall dead.

"It's over. You niggas get on outta here! You did what you came to do. Now git! It's over!" the young man shouted cradling his mother's head in his arms.

Ol' Ben and a couple of others picked me up and threw me over my saddle before racing off with me. An hour or so later we reached Three Winds although I can't recollect what happened after that as I was in out of consciousness.

But I do remember Petunia crying and cursing me at the same time. Awakening the next morning I felt the deep burning in my shoulder and was surprised to find a room full of people standing around the bed.

I tried to move but the pain was too great.

"You be still Andrew!" Petunia said fussing over me and pushing the spoon in my mouth.

"What's wrong? What's all the commotion?" I said looking at the faces of Josiah, Jeremiah, Fiona and Ben.

"You've been shot. From what I understand some old grizzled up eighty year old white woman shot you good," Jeremiah said smiling. "And from what I understand it was a fair fight. You said draw and she outdrew you and then just because she outdrew you in a fair fight Ol' Ben here drew on her and cut her down. That's what folks are saying anyway."

It was all starting to come back to me now. The boy, the farmhouse, everything…

"Did the boy make it?"

"He was the only survivor," Ben said. "If you ask me he should have perished with all the rest. No witnesses. The sheriff's already been around here asking questions but the boy didn't say anything. Say he come home and found them that way. Either he's sincere in wanting this to be over or he's too damn scared to talk. Anyway he claims he don't know nothing and we sho as hell don't know nothing about no mass killing or no farm being burned down to the ground. But don't you worry yo'self none about that. It's like the boy say. It's over. You just rest and let this fine young hammer nurse you back to health son," Ben said flirting with Petunia. "Missed you last night Jeremiah but I guess we did okay without you. Looks like married life is doing alright by you. You picking up a lil weight around the mid-section ain'tcha boy?" he said patting Jeremiah on the back as he grabbed his rifle and headed for the door.

"Come on. All the rest of you out too. Gotta let Andrew get some rest."

I watched as they left and suddenly felt very tired.

Petunia was back within minutes.

"You know this wouldn't have happened if I had been with you don't you?"

"How's that?" I asked smiling and pulling her close to me with my good arm.

"Why I sure wouldn't have let some old gray haired white woman shoot my baby's daddy," she leaning over and kissing me deeply.

21091030R00083

Made in the USA
Middletown, DE
18 June 2015